Whether wispy and ethereal, crisp and graphic or blanket-like and comforting, cloth can speak to us intimately. In this fascinating book, renowned textile artist Hannah Lamb explores the significance behind fabric and its uses in textile art to create richly evocative pieces with deep layers of meaning.

She begins with an introduction to different types of materials, exploring their individual properties and symbolic connotations, and goes on to examine the connection between process and material, focusing on individual techniques such as hand stitch, cyanotype print, surface manipulation, mending and devoré. The text is accompanied by beautiful images throughout, including finished pieces from some of today's best textile artists. This book is the perfect guide for textile artists who want to harness the poetic qualities of fabric and develop a more personal approach to process, material and making.

Poetic Cloth

Hannah Lamb

BATSFORD

Contents

Introduction

Rummaging through boxes in my studio, I soon become distracted. An old paper bag from a department store spills its contents, several metres of ivory wedding dress silk, the pearly smooth surface catching the light as it runs through my hands. Another box reveals fluttering, tissue-like layers of cotton organdie, rolled-up offcuts of Lithuanian linen and, near the bottom, a weighty piece of heavy woollen cloth yields a subtle, earthy aroma of lanolin. As I handle cloth my mind seems to switch to a more sensory and emotional way of thinking. The texture, drape and handle of the cloth, the way it sounds and smells, how light is reflected or absorbed, these are all important aspects of the way it seduces (or repels) us. But beyond that, there are intangible qualities, difficult to put your finger on, that provoke highly personal responses, reminding us of particular places, people and occasions. Materials speak to us if we choose to listen. They speak of touch, memory and place. For me, cloth has the ability to describe what is difficult to put into words – it is poetic.

Cloth is capable of communicating something, far more than simply being a backdrop for surface decoration. It isn't enough to say that you are going to use cotton: what kind? Lightweight or heavy? Canvas, calico, percale or organdie? Freshly starched, or a vintage, washed and worn material? For any artist function plays a part in choosing materials, but it is also important to consider how materials communicate with the viewer. What do we say through our use of materials? In this book I want to share some thoughts on how cloth, stitch and surface can be used to create personal meaning in textile art. It isn't intended as a rule book, but instead aims to unpick some of my own thoughts and personal approaches, which I hope will be helpful to those who are interested in taking a deeper, more thoughtful approach to their own practice.

Grounded in key elements of my textile practice, I begin with an introduction to materials, their properties and symbolic meanings. Subsequent chapters explore the connection between process and material, focusing on hand stitch, cyanotype print, surface manipulation, mending and construction. The emphasis throughout is on sensitivity to material, a quiet attention to detail and thoughtful application of textile technique. I encourage you to explore the ideas in this book in your own way, finding personal approaches to process, material and making.

ABOUT ME

Growing up, I was surrounded by textiles and by people who made things from them, not in any artistic sense but certainly with ingenuity, creativity and great care. During countless trips to wool and fabric shops with my mum, I learnt about different fabrics, how they felt and how they moved. In turn I also learned to sew, to make things (despite the tears and teenage tantrums), and when I studied at art school, it is perhaps not surprising that I turned to textiles as my artistic medium of choice. Today, as a practising artist and lecturer in

textile design, I am immersed in a world of textiles. I am lucky to live and work in the historical heartland of woven wool cloth production – Bradford, West Yorkshire – where the very landscape speaks of cloth. Since moving here 15 years ago, I have been fortunate to work alongside skilled makers, archivists, talented designers and industry experts, and to have become a part of a wider network of textile professionals. My practice has therefore developed in a very personal way in response to the place I live and work in, finding my way in the world through cloth and making. In my teaching, too, I have been lucky to be part of a two-way process of sharing; my students have helped me to question and formulate my practice, and if there is one thing I have realized from all my years of study and teaching, it is that the more I know, the more there is to learn.

The overspilling boxes of cloth in my studio act as a repository for memories, for tactile knowledge and shared material language. By working with that fabric I bring it to life, developing new narratives. For me, cloth is not just the medium I work with, it is the way I think.

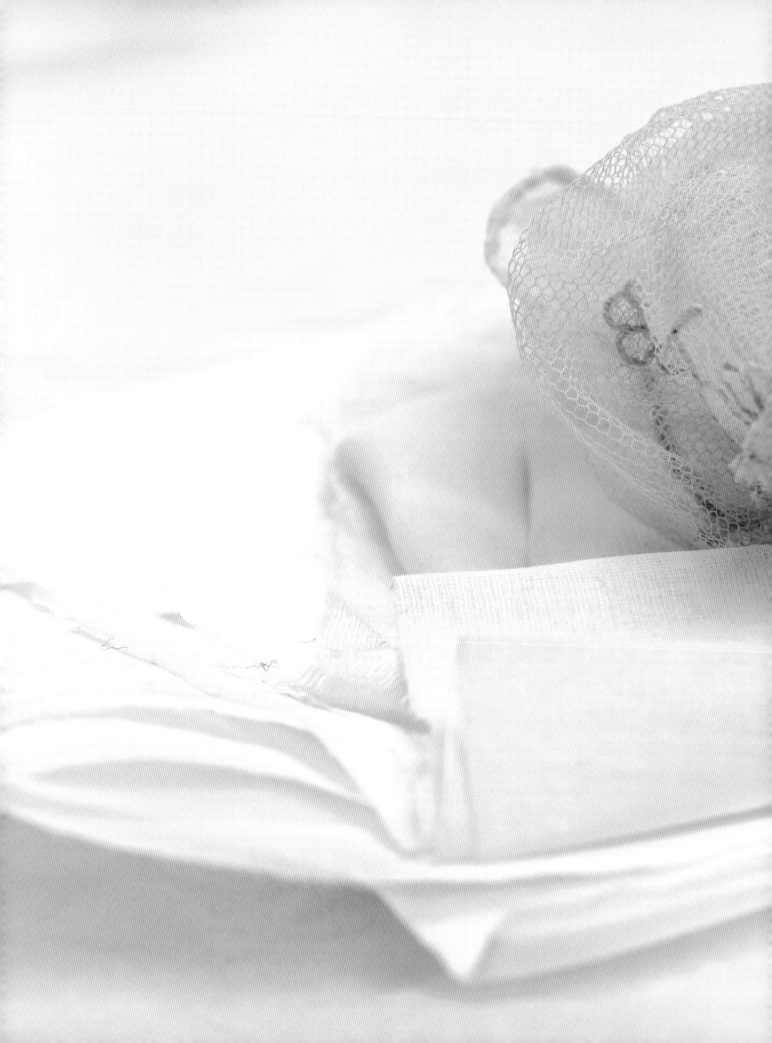

Part One
Touch

Cloth

'The aim of art is to represent not the outward appearance of things, but their inward significance.'[1]

Cloth is our second skin, enfolding and protecting us from cradle to grave. It swaddles and shrouds, keeping us warm, protecting us, providing a barrier between us and the rest of the world. Cloth plays a silent witness to our daily lives, our most intimate, humdrum, celebratory and troubling times. In the context of art, cloth is a highly charged artistic medium. As raw media, paint, pastel, charcoal and bronze do not carry with them the baggage of strong associations and subtle nuances held intrinsically within textiles. Before we make a single stitch, cloth already holds within its folds complex themes around culture, place, politics, gender, memory, birth, sex and death. While we can enhance these ideas through our making processes, the strong symbolism attached to cloth is inherent. Other meanings can be much more personal, resonating from the immediacy of a tactile response, triggering a memory or association. It is this ability to communicate on both a universal and personal level that endows textiles with an important place in contemporary art practice as a medium to express personal narratives, as well as the most pressing matters of our age.

Material significance is highly personal, yet at the same time there are some common cultural meanings associated with certain fabrics. Red and white gingham always reminds me of summer and school uniform dresses. Some fabrics mean certain things to certain groups or generations. My mother pulls a face at the mention of Crimplene, the memory of the spongy synthetic texture hard-wired into her memory, as is the feel of sweat-inducing nylon sheets from the same period. I remember my grandmother fishing out old linen buttons from her button tin and describing the liberty bodice she wore as a young girl. Cloth has powerful associations through memory, in part because of its tactile, sensory nature.

[1] Attributed to Aristotle, as cited in Will Durant, *The Story of Philosophy* (Simon and Schuster, 1926).

MATERIAL QUALITIES

The crispness of starched cotton and the warmth
of a felted woollen blanket have very different
material qualities and meanings: one cool,
smooth, neat; the other warm and comforting.
In our daily lives we understand the properties
of different materials and they help us to find
comfort. In the art world, these ways of
understanding materials are expanded to carry
symbolic meanings.

While some meanings are understood in
cultural contexts, others will have a more personal
significance, perhaps from our memories and
association with certain people, places or times
in our lives. In my own work I tend to gravitate
towards fabrics made from natural fibres,
especially second-hand or vintage materials,
preferring the way they feel in my hand. Silk,
wool, cotton or linen fabrics form the main body
of my palette, with occasional small highlights
of something unexpected, like a metallic thread,
a scrap of something fancy, or a patterned fabric.
I am drawn towards materials with a backstory,
particularly those with some age, which I discuss
in more depth throughout this book.

In the pages that follow I show some of my
favourite materials, collected into groups that are
themed by the qualities and ideas they suggest.

Right: Vintage linen
buttons on their original
shop display card.

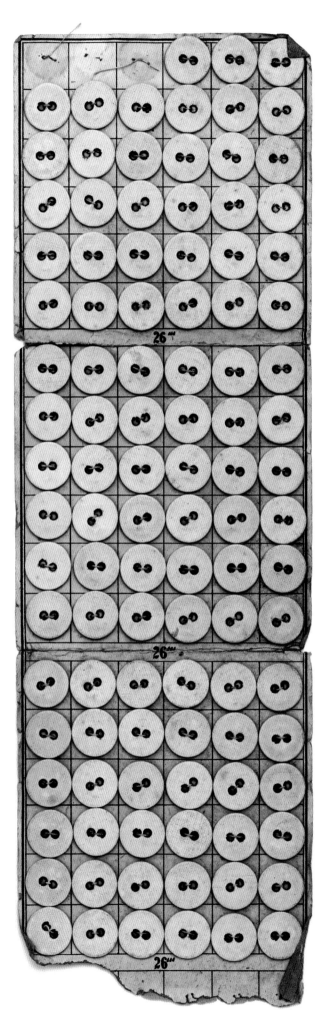

11

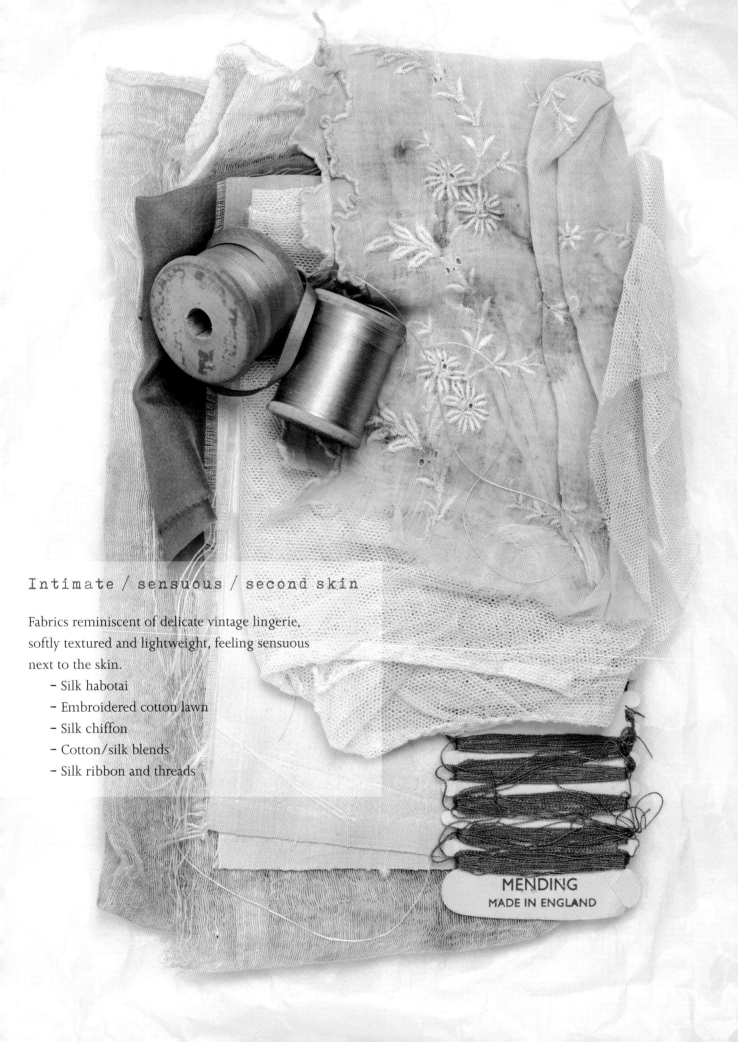

Intimate / sensuous / second skin

Fabrics reminiscent of delicate vintage lingerie,
softly textured and lightweight, feeling sensuous
next to the skin.

- Silk habotai
- Embroidered cotton lawn
- Silk chiffon
- Cotton/silk blends
- Silk ribbon and threads

MENDING
MADE IN ENGLAND

Comfort(ing) / domestic / warm

Softly insulating materials recall the warmth
of traditional quilts and blankets.
Old materials that have been washed and
worn have a humble, lived-in quality.

- Woollen blankets
- Brushed cotton
- Washed and worn prints
- Quilted fabrics
- Patchwork

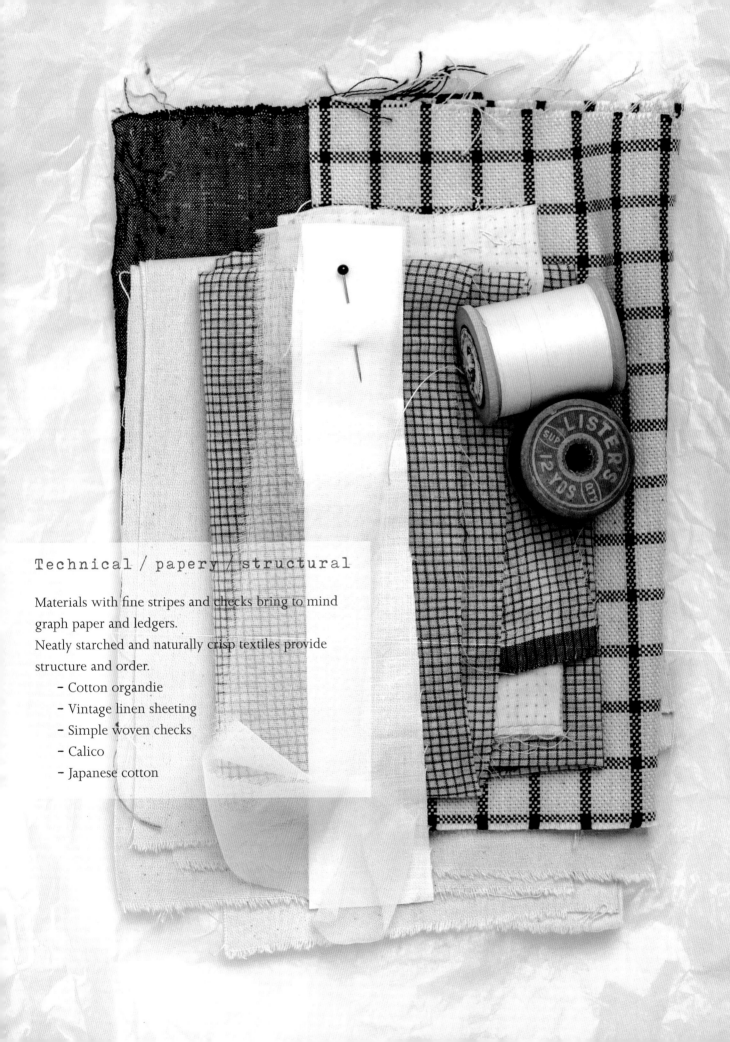

Technical / papery / structural

Materials with fine stripes and checks bring to mind
graph paper and ledgers.
Neatly starched and naturally crisp textiles provide
structure and order.

- Cotton organdie
- Vintage linen sheeting
- Simple woven checks
- Calico
- Japanese cotton

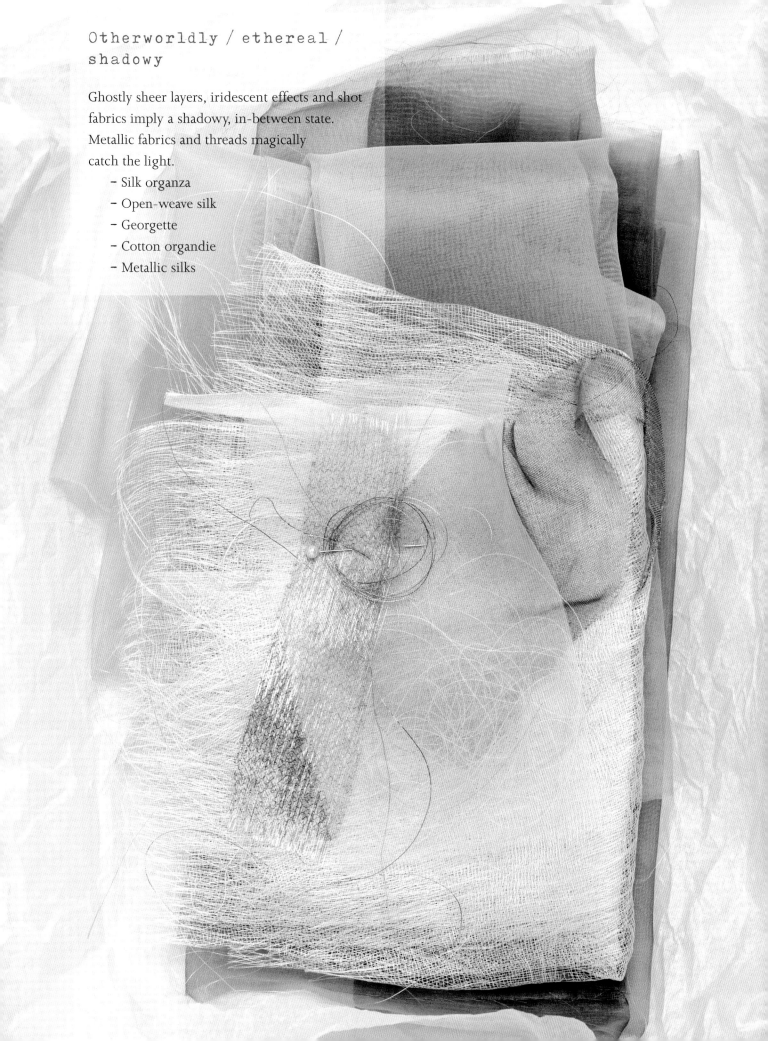

Otherworldly / ethereal / shadowy

Ghostly sheer layers, iridescent effects and shot
fabrics imply a shadowy, in-between state.
Metallic fabrics and threads magically
catch the light.

- Silk organza
- Open-weave silk
- Georgette
- Cotton organdie
- Metallic silks

FIBRE AND FABRIC

As well as considering the meaning and significance of textiles, there are also practical and physical qualities to bear in mind. Materials can be chosen for their texture, transparency, weight, density, drape and structure. Lightweight fabrics convey a lightness of touch, sensitivity and delicacy, while heavyweight materials are weighty, suggesting solidity, structure and mass. While these are all physical properties that can be used in a practical sense, they can also be explored as abstract qualities in your artwork. In projects where I want to explore qualities of light and shadow I always work with very lightweight fabrics, which both allow light to filter through and give a suggestion of lightness. I give a lot of consideration to how a fabric needs to function and what role it has to perform in a project. If I need a strong, sturdy base, I might support the reverse of my work with an old felted wool blanket, or an interlining fabric. On the other hand, if I am looking for a fluid fabric, one that will ripple in a breeze, I might choose a lightweight habotai

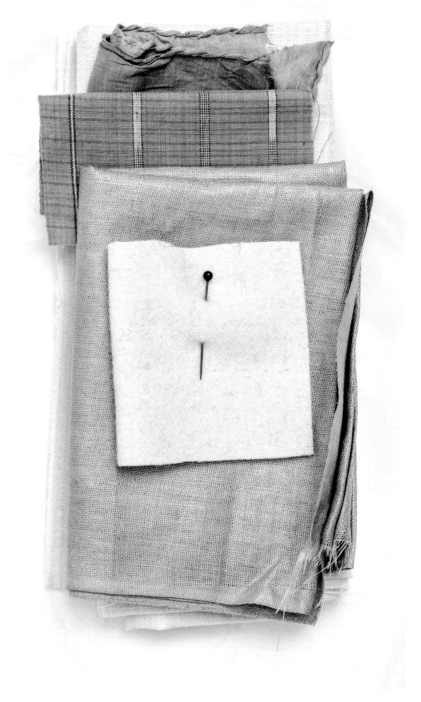

Above: Natural-fibre fabrics, including wool, linen, silk and cotton, all have different properties and uses in my work.

silk. It is also important to be aware of what your materials are made from. Throughout this book you will see that some processes require specific types of fabric or fibre base, especially where dye and print processes are concerned. A simple burn test can be carried out to determine the fibre content of a fabric (see page 120). The main groups of fibre are:

Natural Protein fibres include animal-hair fibres like wool, cashmere, alpaca, angora, mohair and horsehair, and, also in this category, silk created by the silkworm. Plant fibres include cotton, flax (linen), ramie, hemp, jute and less commonly seen fabrics made from nettle, banana and pineapple.

Man-made Usually made from cellulose material like wood pulp and bamboo, man-made or semi-synthetic fibres are heavily processed to create materials described as viscose, rayon, bamboo or by several trade names such as Lyocell, Modal and Tencel.

Synthetic These are fibres made entirely from petrochemicals, and include nylon, polyamide, polyester and elastane.

Non-woven and non-textile materials

In this book I also refer to some non-textile materials that I feel have a strong affinity with cloth, such as leather and paper. As a skin, leather is arguably even closer to us than cloth, while paper (sometimes made of cotton rags) in its sheet form can be stitched and manipulated almost like fabric. Both come in a myriad of different textures, properties and surface finishes, and are capable of conveying a whole range of meanings and associations, just like cloth.

TRUTH TO MATERIALS

This popular principle in 20th-century modernist art, architecture and design held that materials should be used and seen in their raw, unaltered state, embracing their natural or inherent qualities. A good example of truth to materials in modernist architecture, for example, is the use of poured concrete as a building material in its raw state, without painting, cladding or even sanding out the marks of the timber shuttering. The idea is to celebrate the material as it is and even draw attention to the way it has been constructed.

At its core the concept of truth to materials is about the honest use of materials employed with integrity. Aim to choose materials that you enjoy in their own right, in terms of how they feel and that are fit for purpose. Show off the material in its raw state or draw attention to how it has been constructed. This might include leaving seams visible or highlighting construction by using a contrasting colour of thread. It should be emphasized that truth to materials is not about poor craftsmanship; if anything, it is the absolute opposite. When the material and method of construction is on show, it is even more important that they are used with care and intention.

In the chapters that follow we take these ideas about materials into practical methods of making, manipulating and selecting cloth.

Swatch

**Always make sure you are working with good natural daylight
when selecting colours and materials.**

When I start a new project, I enjoy rummaging through boxes of fabrics and threads in the studio to find things that seem right. I very seldom buy an entire new collection of materials for a project. Instead I use what I have as a starting point. Gathering supplies together in a box or basket helps to keep all of the things I am working with together and provides an instant view of my palette of materials.

I find the exercises below helpful when choosing materials, to get a feel for how they work together. If you don't yet have a stash of threads and fabrics, you will probably need to visit a fabric shop or haberdashery to start collecting some supplies. Don't feel shy about taking an image or initial source of inspiration with you; it can save you time, money and disappointment. I sometimes carry a snippet of the specific colour I am searching for in my purse; that way, if I happen upon a good supplier, I have the colour reference to hand. On page 122 I have provided a list of suppliers to get you started.

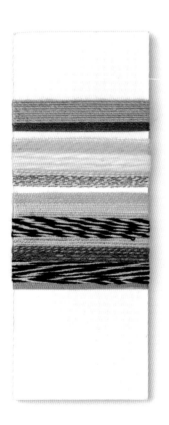

THREAD WRAPS

This exercise is a useful way to start exploring colour for a project. It's a great way to begin colour exploration and material planning, and the finished thread-wrapped card acts as a pocket-sized colour reference when shopping for additional threads and fabrics.

Working from a coloured image or object, select threads or yarns that best match each of the colours you can see. You may find it helpful to focus on a small area of the image by masking it off with strips of paper. Take your time to really look at the colours present. It is important not to jump to conclusions about the colours you expect to see but to truly observe what is in front of you.

Wind the threads around a small piece of cardboard, sticking the thread ends to the back of the card with adhesive tape. As you wind the threads, consider the proportion of colours in

Opposite: As well as matching colours, consider different thicknesses and textures of thread in your wraps.

Above: Objects collected on a misty autumn morning. I collected these as they seemed to reflect the colours I saw in the wider landscape.

your image. Which are the main (dominant) colours? Which colours are only seen in tiny amounts? Try to convey this in how wide your bands of colour are. Continue to select and wind the threads until you have picked out all of the colours.

In the examples shown, I have selected threads based on objects collected on a misty autumn walk.

Further ideas

- Work from the same image again but alter the proportions, or leave out some colours you don't like.
- For complex or flecked colours, twist together different-coloured threads to create a new thread.
- Experiment with different textures, such as fluffy, metallic, shiny or rough-textured yarns.
- Wind over a coloured background – this can help you to visualize how your threads would look on different-coloured base fabrics.

WORD ASSOCIATION

With your project research, images, sketchbook, etc., in front of you, make a list of words that suggest the material qualities you wish to translate. A list from my notebook reads: misty, veiled, greyed colours, ink spots, heathered/blended, autumnal, amber, grey, soft focus, rich colour. Some of these words could describe colours, others textures; most are open to personal interpretation, which is exactly what we want. For me, a misty fabric might be a gauze, or perhaps a lighter fabric, such as a shadowy silk georgette. The blended or 'heathered' colours suggest tweed, while ink spots translate into fabrics and threads with black spots and speckles.

Left: Small swatches of fabrics and threads provide a visual reference for your project.

20

*Above: Fabrics and threads laid out in a
spectrum of graded colours.*

- Misty
- Veiled
- Greyed colours
- Ink spots
- Heathered/
  blended
- Autumnal
- Amber
- Grey
- Soft focus
- Rich colour

Using your own list of words and any of your coloured images as inspiration, start to select from the materials and threads you have to hand. Some fabric shops will give you a small sample swatch for colour matching, which can be helpful to add to what you already have. Lay out the ones that you think work, remembering that not every fabric has to fulfil all of the words. I like to lay out my fabrics neatly in a spectrum of graded colours or tones, placing threads on top. Sometimes the thread acts as an accent colour that lifts an otherwise very similar collection of fabrics. Although usually a bold colour, an accent colour could be of any hue or shade, providing there is a strong contrast between the base fabric and accent stitching.

Once assembled, look at your materials palette. Do the colours and textures represent the 'look' you want to achieve? Is there anything missing? Make a shopping list of things you would like to add. Cut small pieces of the selected fabrics and pin them to a board or your sketchbook page as a visual reference.

SWATCHES AS SAMPLERS

Once you have made your selection of coloured threads and fabrics, you may find it helpful to explore how they work together in different combinations.

Cut small swatches from your fabrics and lay them on a neutral backing fabric, such as natural calico or white cotton sheeting. Experiment with overlapping patches of different materials in differing proportions to create mini colour groups, leaving some space around each group. Create different variations on your colour palette, making each grouping distinct. This could be achieved by using a different dominant colour or by varying how many of the colours you use in each group. Take short lengths of your threads and place them on top of different fabrics, experimenting with combinations to create harmony or dynamic accents.

Stand back a little. Try shutting one eye and squinting with the other (I find this gives me an overview of my work without fussing over details). Does anything stand out as odd? Is there anything missing? Does it feel like a unified palette?

When you are happy with the results, secure the fabrics in place with a repositionable spray fabric glue (such as 505 Spray and Fix) or pins.

If you wish you can now explore how different threads combine with your fabrics by adding stitch. This can present some surprising results. Use stitches that run across different areas rather than sewing around the edges, as this will help you to see how a thread changes its appearance against different textures and colours. Use simple stitches like running stitch or stem stitch. Try a single line of stitch that runs across different fabrics, or an area scattered with seeding stitches, and see if you can blend from one colour to another.

Opposite: On this sampler I have begun the stitching process, testing a few of my threads with different fabric groups.

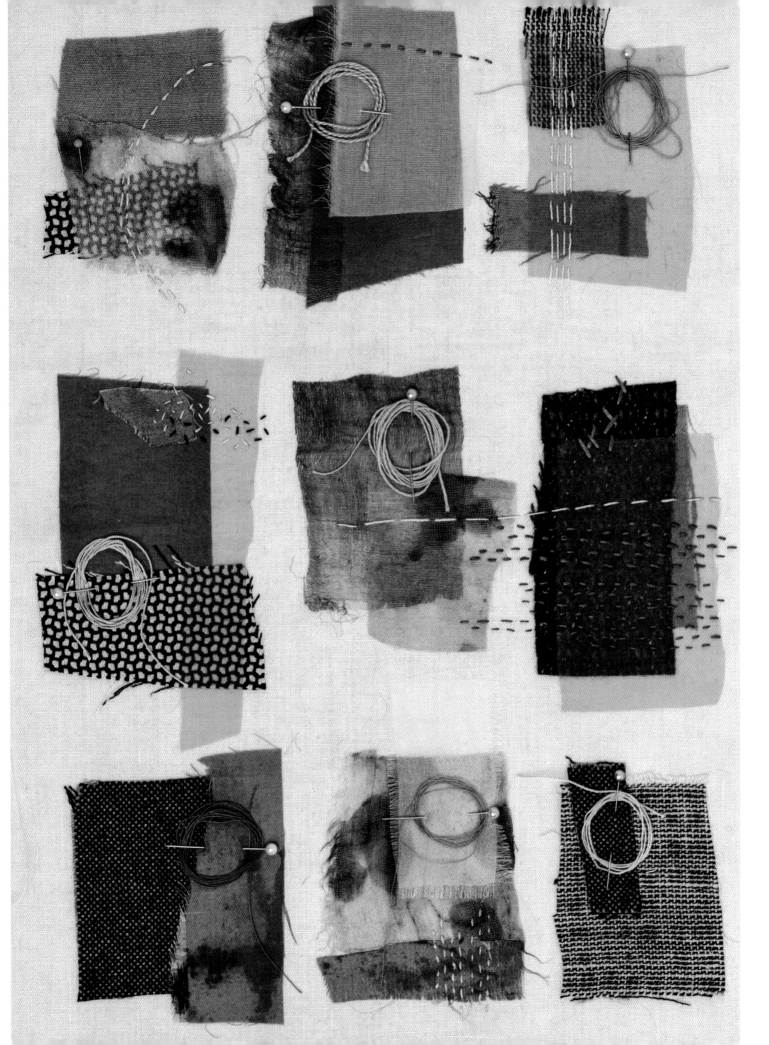

Part Two
Stitch

Mark

**'Rather than think of stitches as separate from each other,
their movements allow for the exploration of marks on various fabrics ...
the practice of stitching and the movements involved relate
to the migration of peoples and stitches ...'[2]**

Stitch, when used in an art textiles context, can be applied like a mark made in any other artistic medium, such as paint or charcoal; and, just like those other artistic mark-making media, with practice stitch can become an intuitive and natural part of our visual vocabulary. While this might sound intimidating, if you think about the kind of doodles you might make in the margins of a notebook, these are instinctive marks created without overthinking. Study any book of embroidery stitches and you will probably see several that could be used to create similar impressions.

My art school education inspired me to draw freely with expressive marks, interpreting my ideas and the world around me. Likewise, my embroidery training encouraged me to create a wide range of marks with stitch, uninhibited by formality and developed in a way that expressed my own eye and hand.

If you are new to embroidery, I recommend practising a selection of stitches until you feel comfortable working them with ease. The more comfortable you are working stitches, the more intuitive you can be when using them in your work. As a starting point, it can be helpful to choose a few basic stitches, for example, running stitch, chain stitch and French knot. Make a sampler of each stitch, testing out different threads and changing the scale of your stitches, from tiny to huge. On each sampler, experiment with variations of those stitches: try changing the spacing, stacking stitches closer together, opening the stitch out, or stretching the start or end point. Worked in this way, stitches can evolve into your own personalized stitches or migrate into other known stitches; for example, an opened-out chain stitch can become what we understand as a single feather stitch. Anne Butler Morrell's extensive study of global stitch traditions has identified the extent to which stitches are interrelated, and she suggests that they can be better understood in terms of the movement made to achieve them.

Inspired by this unrestrictive understanding of stitch forms, I have always encouraged my students to be inventive with their stitches. While it can be helpful to name specific stitches, it is also important to recognize that most stitches have a variety of names and variations across the many different

---

[2] Anne Butler Morrell, *The Migration of Stitches & the Practice of Stitch as Movement* (D.S. Mehta/Sarabhai Foundation, 2007).

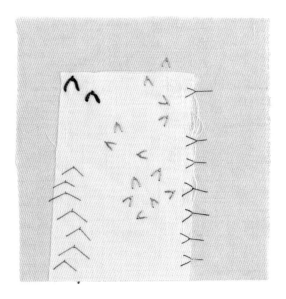
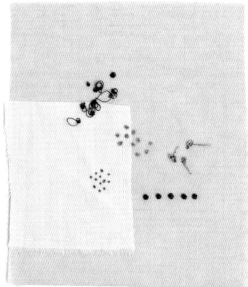
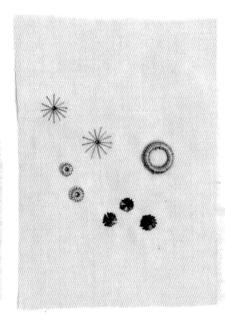

embroidery categories and traditions. The same stitch can even have different names when worked on transparent fabric, even-weave linen, or with the addition of embellishments. For example, a stitch defined by a simple in-and-out action can be a running stitch on a single piece of cloth, used temporarily as a tacking stitch, or used to join two pieces together as a seam, and furthermore it can be repeated over an area as a darning stitch or used to stitch down beads as a beading stitch. In the art textiles context, there is no need to be bound by traditional forms and definitions of embroidery: you are free to use stitches in your own way to express your ideas.

Over the years I have favoured a group of stitches that I use widely in my work, altering them to the specific project in hand. Some of these can be used as individual marks, some as different kinds of linear mark, and others as filling stitches to cover areas (see page 32). Some stitches are very adaptable and can be used in several ways. Each person needs to find their own stitch vocabulary: a set of stitches and variations that form personal meaning for them.

Above: Experimental samplers exploring (from left) fly stitch, French knot and eyelet stitches.

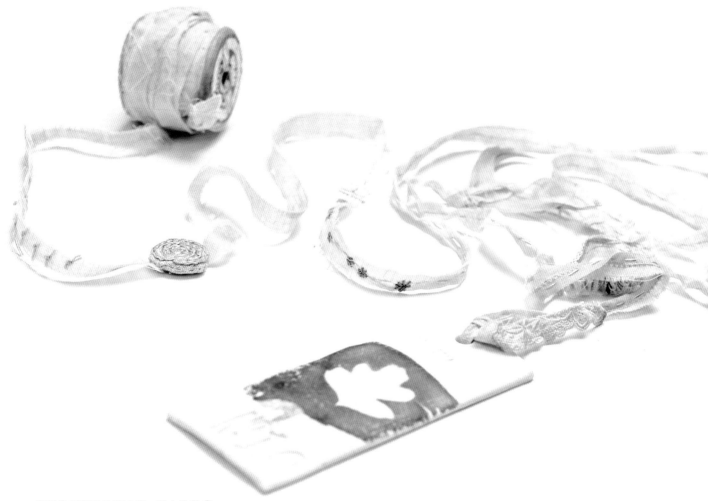

INDIVIDUAL MARKS

Used on their own, some stitched marks can be worked to create a kind of visual punctuation. Rather than creating an outline or used to colour in an area, individual marks are highlights, accents or even signatures. They are intended to stand out, to make their mark. As in writing, I use stitched marks as a focal or stopping point. A French knot, woven wheel, eyelet stitch, or other circular mark can successfully draw the eye, like a full stop. A fly stitch is more open but can also be used effectively on its own or in small groups, and where it is made with a long stalk, the eye will tend to follow the direction of the stitch.

There are also some useful parallels with maps, where symbols are used to denote specific things in the landscape. In this way, you can choose to create your own visual language of marks in your work. In my installation work *Linear Mapping*, I used individual stitch marks to symbolize things I saw or experienced in the landscape. Each ribbon or thread represents a walk I made, my stitches recording the sounds of birdsong, the colour of distinctive plants, or even the weather. Tiny, rosette-like stitches were made in response to the contrast between the pale, drab leaf litter of a woodland floor and the vibrant green moss I spotted growing in clumps. Used like this, stitches become personalized mapping symbols, marking a point in time and place.

Above: **Linear Mapping** *(2015). Detail of installation. Porcelain, textiles, cyanotype and hand stitch.*

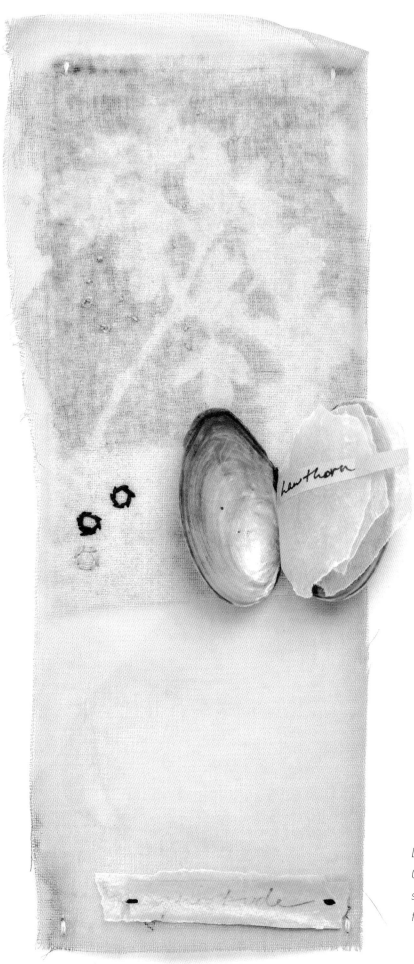

Left: **Quietude** *(2012).*
Cyanotype and hand
stitch. Cotton, wool and
freshwater clam shell.

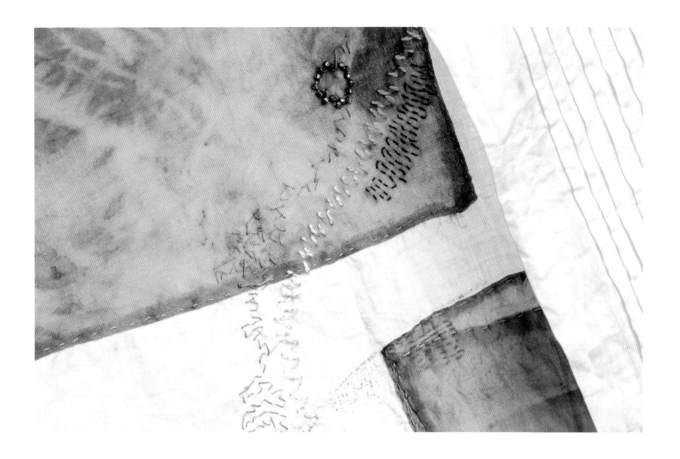

LINEAR STITCHES

Another group of stitches that have a resonance with mapping are the linear stitches. Running stitch, back stitch and double back stitch (or closed herringbone), and variations on those stitches, all remind me of different ways of moving through the landscape. As I recall my route across the land, I stitch lines of travel across the cloth. By varying the thread, the stitch length and the gaps between, I evoke tentative steps through deep undergrowth or confident strides along established footpaths. The stitch paths might follow contours or go around obstacles; sometimes I retrace my steps. It isn't always important to me that someone else will understand my stitch marks in exactly the same way as I do; it is much more important that I express my idea in a way that means something to me.

In the image above, I used stitch to mark the memory of a walk. The stitches recall the walk in local woodland and along the river, either mapping my route or recording observed features and sensory experiences. The stitches are abstract and symbolic rather than representational, acting as a memory trigger that I recognize and which helps to anchor that experience in my memory.

Above: **In Search of Green** *(2013). Detail of installation.*
Opposite, left: **Imprint II** *by Caroline Bartlett. Detail.*
Opposite, right: **Pulse** *by Caroline Bartlett.*

Caroline Bartlett

Describing cloth as a 'repository of memory', Caroline Bartlett's practice explores 'the historical, social and cultural associations of textiles, their significance in relation to touch and their ability to trigger memory and speak of identity'. This is seen in the richly layered, tactile qualities of *Pulse* and *Imprint*, in which the densely pleated and dyed cloth surrounds a central embossed porcelain disk. Stitching punctuates both textile and ceramic, the thread creating marks on the surface and issuing forth from the piece. Caroline describes her practice as a process of 'imprinting, stitching, erasing, reworking and folding', and while her process now has a strong emphasis on stitch, her print training is evident in the way that marks appear almost as an imprint or impression in cloth.

'Fragile and transient, cloth encapsulates ideas concerned with the regenerative and degenerative processes of life. As clothing, it witnesses routines, rituals and intimacies. The clothing-imprinted porcelain occurs as a deposit of memory, the circular pleating references life's experiences folding backwards and forwards. This motion is replicated in the working process.'

Surface

One of the many things I love about hand stitch is the diversity of marks that can be created and the multitude of ways in which they can be utilized to express ideas. A row of running stitches can be used to trace a tentative, barely visible line on cloth; however, the same basic stitch, repeated in rows across an area, starts to build up a new surface that integrates those stitches with the body of the fabric and a new, one-of-a-kind cloth emerges.

In embroidery terms, stitches used to cover an area are often described as filling stitches because they can be used to fill a shape. I sometimes use filling stitches in this way to create a contained area of marks or for surface texture. An area of seeding is a very effective way of playing with texture and colour.

FILLING WITH SEEDING

For this technique you may find it helpful to stretch lightweight fabric in a hoop or embroidery frame to provide tension. Start by defining the area or shape you wish to fill with a line of tacking stitches (these will be removed afterwards). Seeding is worked by making small individual stitches of the same length in random directions, gradually building up to evenly cover an area with stitches, just like scattering seed evenly across newly prepared soil. This can be done in a single colour of thread, or with a mixture of colours to create a blended effect.

Dot stitch can be worked in a very similar way, the double stitch on the same spot simply making a more defined, often raised, mark.

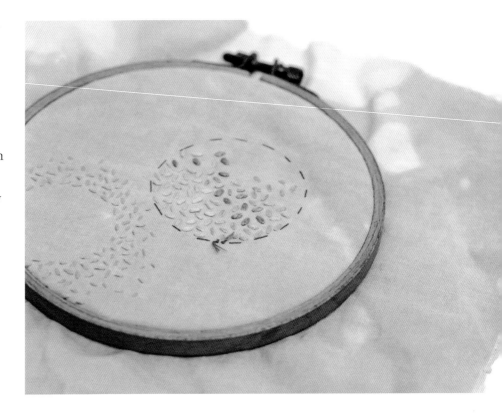

Right: Seeding worked inside a circle of tacking stitches.

Above: **In Search of Green** *(2013). Detail of installation. Seeding stitches can also be used to define a 'negative space' by working around the outside of a shape and blending outwards.*

33

STITCHING ACROSS SURFACES

While traditionally filling stitches are used to fill a contained shape, I also like to use stitch to work across a surface in a more organic, fluid way. Stitches can be scattered across a cloth lightly, condensed in a focused patch, or worked across a wider area with uneven edges that blend with the surrounding areas. Stitches such as seeding, dot stitch, detached chain stitch (or lazy daisy) and darning stitch all lend themselves to these approaches. Worked in this way, stitches can be used to subtly alter the colour of the cloth, remembering that the thread colour may blend with the eye when seen from a distance, just like brush strokes in a painting.

Small, scattered stitches are effective when used to add a dappled effect to a cloth. I like to use this approach to blend areas or to break up the defined edge of a print or patterned fabric. Darning or running stitches worked across an area can also be used to create a similar effect. The versatility of the running stitch, which becomes a darning stitch when woven in and out of the weave of the cloth or a quilting stitch when worked through layers, has been widely exploited in contemporary Western art textiles in recent years. Used in different forms, the basic in-and-out motion of a stitch, worked in rows across a fabric, can be seen in many stitch cultures around the world.

In my own practice, I use rows of running or darning stitches, either on a single piece of cloth or more often through various layers, as a means of consolidating and settling things together. On a practical level, the stitching can help to stabilize fragile fabrics that have started to disintegrate, the stitches holding the delicate fabric and backing it with something more substantial (see page 65). Old woollen blankets, cotton 'bump', or a strong linen fabric can act as a backing for delicate old materials in need of support, and tacking the layers together before starting the darning stitches avoids the movement and distortion of the fabric. The second row of stitches should be offset from the first, and each subsequent row should continue in this pattern, so that the fabric is evenly secured. I must admit that my stitches are seldom entirely even or regular. I don't aim for perfection, looking instead for my stitches to sit organically as part of an evolving cloth story.

When worked across the joins between patches of cloth, darning stitches can also help to blur the boundaries between different materials, giving a softer appearance. Repetitive rows of stitching, built up in this way, help to

Above: **In Search of Green** *(2013). Detail of hand-stitched seeding and darning in silk thread onto cyanotype-printed cotton.*

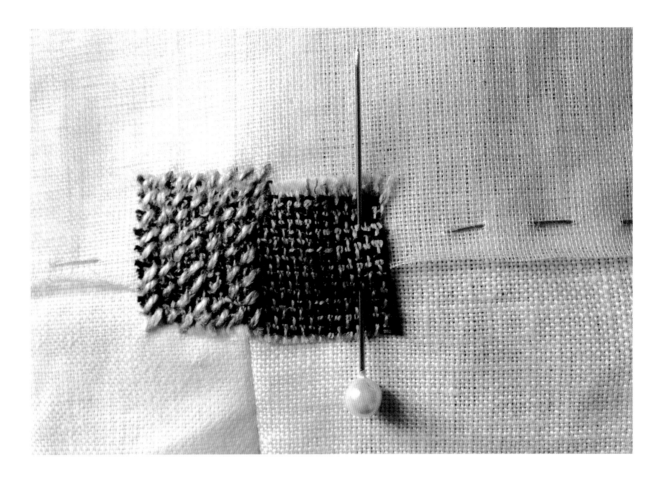

create harmony by bringing together different elements in an artwork; colours become mingled, materials stabilized and the work more unified as a whole. This functions on both a physical and conceptual level. Distinct elements or ideas within a work can be united by stitches that merge.

Above: Tent stitch worked over a patch of coloured woven cloth using variegated cotton thread.

STITCHING IN BLOCKS

More commonly associated with canvas work, tent stitch (which is basically half a cross stitch) is more versatile than you might imagine. I use it to convey a sense of order and repetition, as in the piece shown above, inspired by archival research at Sunny Bank Mill. Weave structures, architectural elements and archival documents influenced my choice of blocks of stitch. Worked on top of a patch of coloured fabric, in some areas the structure of the cloth was used as a guide to keep the stitches fairly regular, and helps to define the area of stitch. It was also a great way to create a blended colour, as the eye seems to mix the colour of stitches with the ground fabric. Using a variegated thread allows for more subtlety of colour.

Claire Wellesley-Smith

Based on the outskirts of Bradford, West Yorkshire, Claire Wellesley-Smith is an artist who enjoys responding to the political and historical landscape around where she lives. Through her 'Slow Stitch' practice, she creates work with careful attention to making and material, aware of a resonance with her surroundings. Her choice of slow-paced hand stitch, combined with a focus on natural dyes sourced on site, heightens her awareness of place and time, creating a mindful approach to making.

Of her artwork *Resist*, she says: 'In 1917, three thousand women marched for peace through central Bradford, a demonstration against the ongoing carnage of the First World War. I used found material from a route that included areas of industrial textile production, now brownfield sites. This material included textile scraps, plant material turned into textile dyes, and metals used as resist prints. Embedded in each textile are hundreds of running stitches using old silk thread from a local mill. I was minded of the repetitious processes of the industries the women kept going during the war: munitions work, weaving cloth for military uniforms. My stitches produced their own rhythm, much like walking, each stitch offering a mark of resistance.'

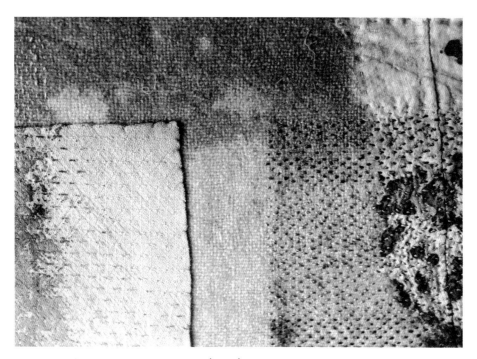

Above: **Resist – Providence Street** *(2017) by Claire Wellesley-Smith. Dyed and stitched cloth.*

Space

In art, composition is a term that refers to how the parts of an artwork are arranged. Each artwork is a composite of different elements, combined to create a particular effect. Sometimes these elements might be distinctive motifs, shapes or objects; at other times they might be different colours, materials or surface qualities. These parts could be combined in a myriad of different ways, and each of those alternatives would look different, and possibly communicate different meanings.

Composition is one of the most important aspects of my practice and I spend a lot of time playing with arrangements, experimenting with different compositions until I find something that seems right. Some people like to create a sketch or design based on initial drawings or other visual inspiration, others make a collage of design elements on paper. Either approach can be effective, and it is really down to personal preference, to how you like to work. I tend to find it easiest to use actual components or materials, making bits, moving them around, pinning in position, cutting bits off, until I am happy with the result. But how exactly do you know when you have a good layout? From years of experience in my own practice and from learning from the work of other artists, I have developed my own idea of what makes a successful composition. Below are some insights into my approaches and thought processes.

SILENT SPACES

In any art form it can be said that the empty spaces are as important as the active elements. Think of a novel and the way that a writer leaves aspects to our imagination, providing just the right amount of description to allow us to build our own picture from the parts we are given while adding our own interpretation to the narrative. Likewise, in the visual arts, the artist can only provide so much. Viewers must bring their own experiences to the work, and therefore one artwork can be seen in a slightly different way by each person as we add our own meaning, based on our own culture, personality, life experiences, likes and dislikes.

One of the hallmarks of my practice is my use of space. I spend a lot of time developing the best composition for a piece, leaving plenty of open, uncluttered space. This suits my style and the ideas that interest me. By leaving blank areas of empty fabric, rather than covering every surface, I create space to rest. These blank spaces act as a counterbalance to areas of detail. Like a pause or brief moment of silence in a musical composition, the space is important in understanding the active elements of the work, marking where something begins and ends, highlighting a powerful section next to it, or just giving room to collect our thoughts and process meaning. For me, silence equals space and space equals silence. It's a pause, a deep breath, before continuing. It's an opportunity to create some stillness, perhaps some peace.

DRAWING THE EYE

One important role of composition is how it helps our eyes travel around an image, creating a sense of order or hierarchy. As a basic rule, the larger the element or motif, the more it will dominate a piece. Things placed in the centre of an artwork will also tend to draw the attention first, especially if they are in a dominant colour or cover a larger area. For example, a big red cross stitched in the centre of a white cloth would draw the eye straight away to that area and nowhere else. The red cross would have a bold impact, but it would not hold the gaze, unless there is other detail to find in the work. The eye very quickly becomes bored and wants to move off to look at something else. How fickle we are!

But what if we want the viewer to spend more time looking and making sense of the narrative in our work? How do we allow the eye to travel across and draw connections between things? Looking at repeat patterns in textile design, you will notice that many use underlying diagonal lines and arrangements to create dynamic compositions (think of traditional floral chintz fabrics). Diagonal lines seem to create energy in an artwork or design, and, in the case of repeat patterns, this helps to distract from the fact that the design has a repeating block. The use of curved or diagonal lines of stitching creates a dynamic movement, while horizontal or vertical lines or arrangements are ordered and more static. Meandering stitch lines encourage us to follow fluid routes through the composition, finding restful spaces and areas of detail to focus on.

Above: A fragment of early 19th-century block-printed chintz.

FOCUSING ON DETAILS

Details are important in composition as they give us a focal point. In a large composition, I sometimes choose to draw attention to a specific part of a much larger image by adding stitch for emphasis. Sometimes I want the eye to be drawn away from the main image, to travel and see other parts. Again, small areas of detailed stitch, or even appliqué patches, provide a point of interest for the eye to linger on. Drawing the eye to a focal point can also be achieved with converging or crossing lines of stitch, or even by using a very small amount of a strong or bright accent colour (as we saw in Swatch in Part One).

TWO-LINE COMPOSITIONS

This simple but effective exercise will allow you to quickly try out a variety of compositions on paper by creating a series of thumbnail sketches.

First, roughly sketch out a series of rectangles in a notebook – there is no need to use a ruler. Using a fine line pen, felt-tip or marker pen, mark just two straight lines on each rectangle. Each rectangle must use a different composition. Start with horizontal and vertical lines, moving on to diagonals, then combining them. See how many different variations you can create.

After you feel you have exhausted the options, stand back from the compositions. Which are the boldest? Which are calming or restful? Are there any you really don't like? Which is your favourite? Remember, these simple two-line compositions are not designed to be finished compositions, but rather to give you an idea about how you might group or arrange stitch motifs in your work and the impact they might create. I generally find off-centre compositions more restful on the eye, and you will see that I use this a great deal in my work.

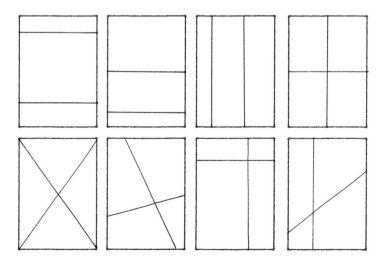

Left: Some of the variations possible with just two lines.

Further ideas

- Try colouring in sections of your drawing, or draw the line with coloured pens.
- Experiment with curved or meandering lines.
- Work on cloth, stitching lines with simple running stitch or back stitch.

DEVELOPING AN EYE FOR COMPOSITION

Next time you visit a gallery, make yourself aware of how you look at a piece of art. Spend some time standing in front of an artwork and notice where your eyes go to. You might find it helpful to soften your gaze or close one eye and squint. Did you see the whole thing at once? Did your eye travel across to different elements of the work? Which parts stood out immediately and which parts did you only notice after a while? By observing things such as these in other people's artwork, I find I become more aware of them in my own.

Below: Stitched two-line compositions.

Dorothy Caldwell

Canadian artist Dorothy Caldwell uses her work to investigate 'how people mark the land and how we come to know "place" through personal landmarks and conventional mapping'.

Her practice involves working on site in remote locations, where 'a personal sense of place is arrived at through walking, gathering, touching and recording'. Initially small on-site responses are made with materials found on the land, which 'reflect the intimate experience of place'. The on-site explorations provide a basis for the large-scale works, 'extending the intimate to include the larger landforms of these vast and silent landscapes'. It is this sense of the small-scale 'intimate' mark from the land, seen as part of a vast landscape, which she makes sense of so beautifully in the large-scale textile pieces. At first glance the work appears as one vast cloth, and then we see that it is in fact made up of an infinite number of smaller elements, constructing a complex whole. Her compositions cleverly use small blocks of colour, along with graphic mark and line to draw the viewer's eye.

Her making 'vocabulary' is drawn from everyday textile traditions such as stitching, darning, mending and patching. She says, 'I approach my cloth as something that needs to be repaired. Like the marks on the landscape, these processes encode a sense of time and history.'

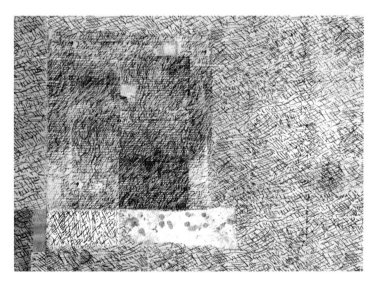

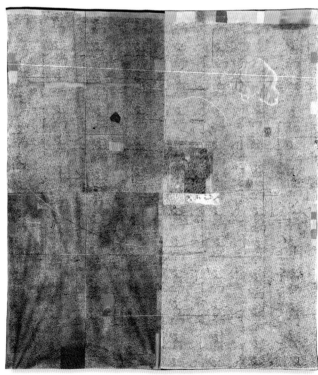

Above: **Map with No Words** *(2013) by Dorothy Caldwell. Detail. Right:* **Map with No Words** *(2013) by Dorothy Caldwell. Silk screen and inkwash on cotton with stitching and appliqué. 285 x 259cm (112 x 102in).*

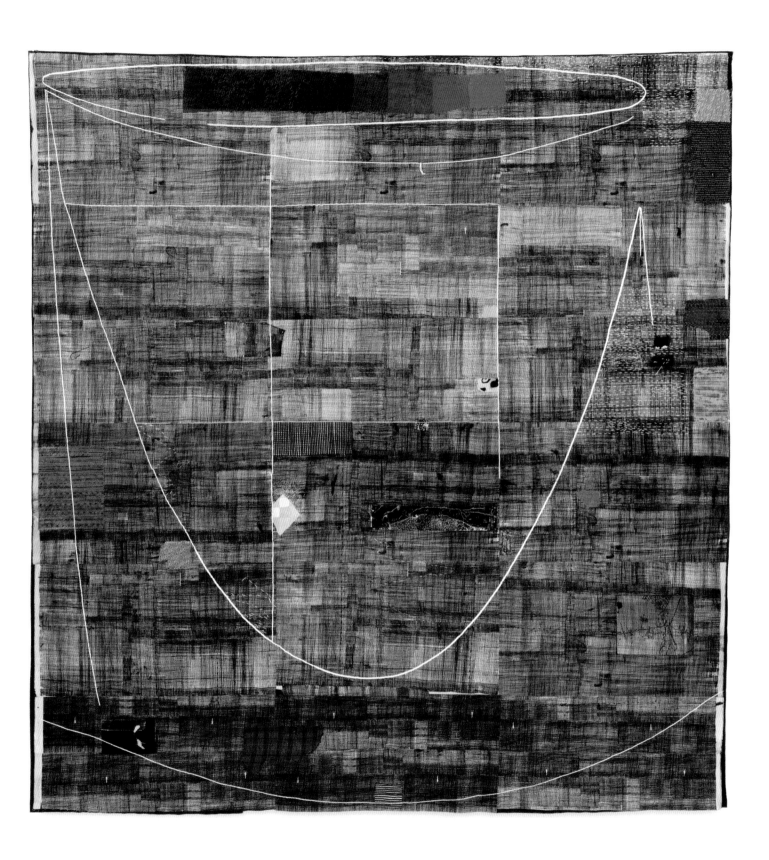

Above: **Fjord** *by Dorothy Caldwell. Wax and silk screen resist on cotton, discharged with stitching and appliqué. 259 x 265cm (102 x 104in).*

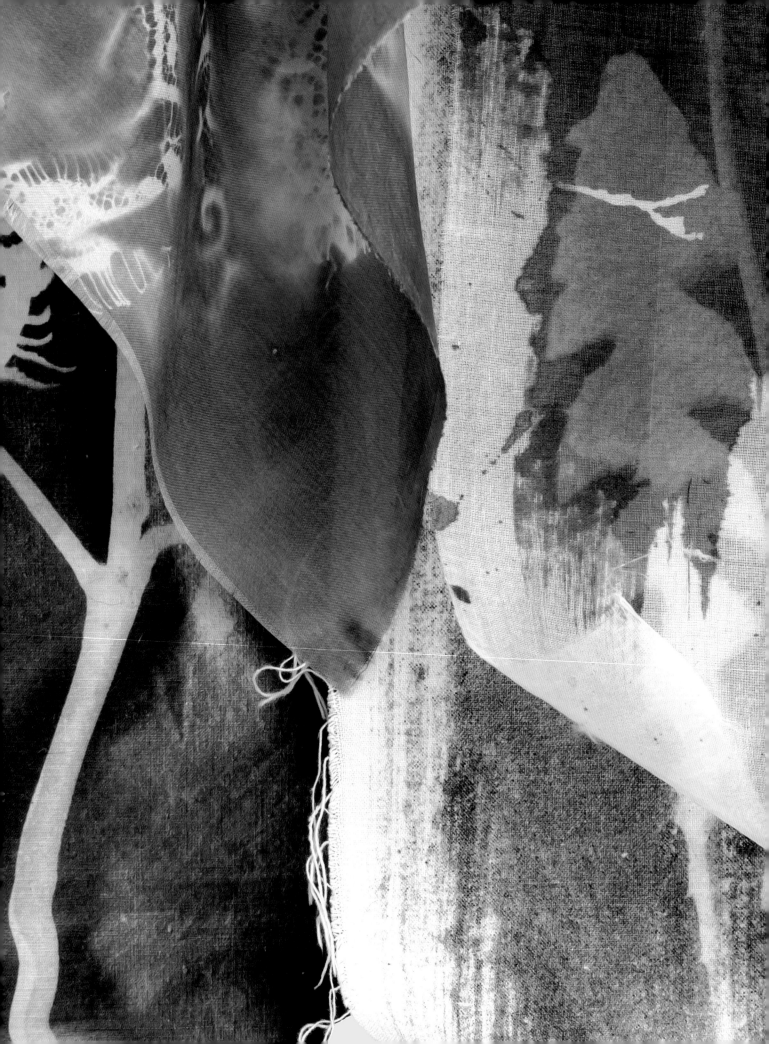

Part Three
Trace

Transparent

Transparent and translucent textiles have a wonderful ability to convey different moods and also to obscure. They partially conceal while offering tantalizing glimpses of what lies beneath. To some, sheer fabrics suggest a close, perhaps sensual connection to the skin. Even the names sound seductive – chiffon, voile, organza, georgette, tulle, mesh – conjuring delicate wisps of cloth that are purely for pleasure. While the veiling and shrouding effect of transparent materials can seduce, it can also give rise to ambiguity, confusion, even disorientation. Through the fog of fibres our view is clouded and distorted, we cannot be sure of what we see. Layers of tissue-like fabric suggest flux or transition, perhaps from one state to another, or between time and place. Shadowy materials perfectly translate a blurring of boundaries.

I am always drawn to the subtle play of light on and through different material surfaces, like low autumn light filtered through a dust-covered window. Light percolating through cloth can have an almost magical, transformative effect. It is this quality that most commonly draws me to work with transparent materials. I love to explore the possibilities of manipulating and stitching cloth, then holding it up to the light to see it transformed.

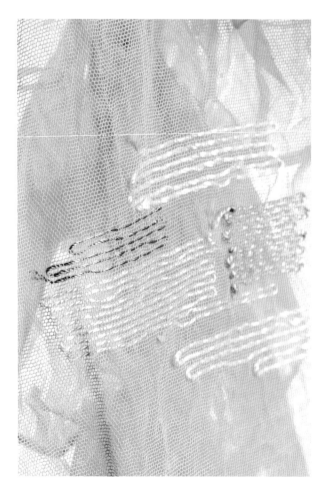

The contrast of transparency against denser areas of stitch or cloth has a strong appeal. This subtle effect reminds me of the dappled light through trees or dancing shadows on my bedroom wall when I was a child, and I have always found it both blissfully calming and enlivening.

While most transparent and semi-transparent fabrics are comprised of very fine threads, others gain their see-through quality from their open construction, such as net and mesh fabrics. Voile, muslin, organdie and organza are plain woven fabrics, varying vastly in drape and stiffness, while the crêpe weave of georgette and chiffon gives a slightly rough texture, which drapes rather beautifully. Cotton organdie has wonderful properties for holding structure, while also being

Right: Darning stitches on net in silk and rayon threads.

46

Above: **In Search of Green** *(2013). Detail of installation.*

quite transparent. Fine cotton lawn is also a pleasure to work with. I search out fine vintage cotton undergarments for their fabric. Transparent fabrics can be made of almost any fibre, including cotton, silk, wool, nylon, acetate and polyester, as well as mixed fibres. They can also include metallic threads, which add a scintillating glint.

Created at the end of a long cold winter, *In Search of Green* was inspired by my search for signs of spring along riverside and woodland paths near my home. The colours echo the change from a snowy landscape to the most delicate traces of green, winter fading as spring emerges. The installation work comprises a series of garments, suggesting my own human presence in the landscape. Sections of delicate Victorian and Edwardian underclothes were pieced together with naturally dyed cloth, and printed and stitched fabrics. The incredibly fragile piece shown here was made from a vintage silk and cotton chemise, the disintegrating silk chiffon ruffles barely holding together at the seams. In places, subtle lines of white and green darning stitches were woven into the fine web of cotton bobbinet at the back of the garment, and the stitches almost seem to hang in space. A tiny feather, printed with cyanotype, is stitched at the neckline. The effect of the piece is of a faint presence, a mere ghost of a cloth, casting a hazy shadow on the wall. The overall impression is ephemeral, cobweb-like, here today and gone tomorrow.

STITCHING SHADOWS

The delicate qualities of translucent materials lend themselves to conveying complex layers of meaning with great subtlety. They also provide some interesting possibilities for hand stitching. You will notice that if you stitch through transparent materials, the thread at the back of the work is visible. This provides scope to create stitches that appear to float in thin air, as well as interesting layered effects. One of the names for this kind of work is 'shadow work', although in India this is known as *chikan* or *chikankari*. The main stitch traditionally used in shadow work is double back stitch or closed herringbone, which is actually just the same stitch worked from the other side. In traditional shadow work most of the stitching is on the back of the piece, but with light behind it, the whole structure of the stitches becomes visible through the cloth.

While double back stitch is particularly successful for shadow work, there is no need to limit yourself to just this one stitch. A simple darning stitch worked across net or mesh fabric can be extremely effective as there is little distinction between the thread on the back and the front of the material. The stitch appears to be suspended in space, a loosely filled area of snaking thread. I like the way this stitch creates areas of density in the cobweb-like fabric.

Right: A chikan embroidered muslin from The Textile Fabrics of India, Vol. VII: Muslins Plain and Embroidered, *c.1866. Bradford College Textile Archive.*

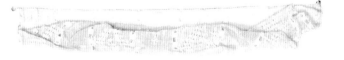

SHADOW STITCH SAMPLING

Experimentation with different stitches on transparent fabrics will reveal the possibilities of shadow stitching. In the samples shown below I have explored a variety of stitches. These include dot stitch used as seeding, which creates organic or random effects, and tent stitch and cross stitch, which appear more orderly. Variations on herringbone and Cretan stitch, either in neat rows or more randomly placed, also offer interesting results. In my samples you can see how changing the scale of the stitches, their spacing and density, can vary the effect of the stitch. The choice of thread is also a big factor. Here I have worked with silk and cotton threads of different thicknesses, some shiny and some matte, which dramatically alter the effect, as does the transparency of the fabric.

When stitching on sheer fabrics, pay particular attention to where the thread travels across the back of the work. If you want an even effect, be consistent in how you work each stitch. I like to hold my work up to a window periodically to see how it appears against the light. Care is also needed at the start and end of your stitching, and I generally find working a tiny back stitch underneath where the first stitch will be placed is the best solution. Occasionally I resort to a small knot when the thread is too bouncy for anything else. Take care that the fabric does not distort as you work. I like to put my work in an embroidery hoop or frame to provide tension and avoid the fabric pulling up; another option is to support your work with soluble fabric, which can be washed away afterwards.

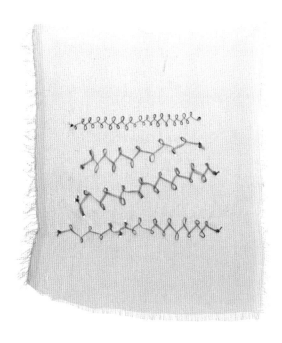

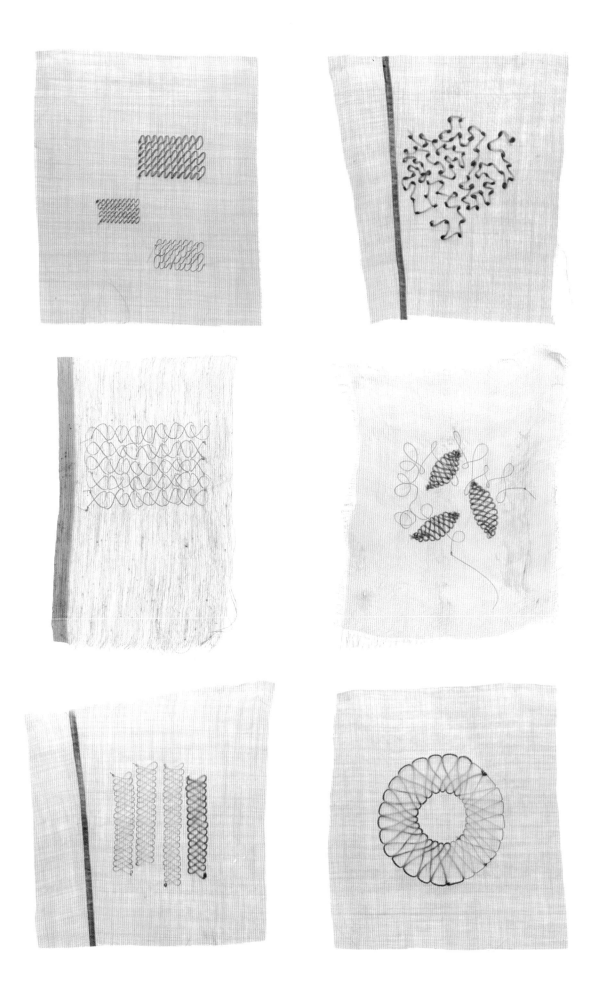

Amanda Clayton

Renowned for her delicate work with white-on-white stitch and transparent material, in her recent work Amanda Clayton explores the narrative possibilities of these fabrics in new, perhaps less decorative ways. In her *Alzheimer's* series, the artist deliberately exploits the qualities of transparent textiles to suggest changing states of mind and consciousness. In the piece *12/13ths asleep*, she describes the effects of *Alzheimer's* as 'never completely shutting off immediate surroundings, that have begun to be frightening and not the same, even by sleeping'. These qualities of instability have been emphasized by using 'different qualities of sheer cloth, folding and hand stitched'. Material choices are important to the meaning in her work, for example introducing a darker contrasting tone 'to represent the 1/13th that keeps awake'. A shifting ambiguity is seen not only in the misty fabric, but also in the format of the work, as she explains, 'Serendipity plays a part as this piece has an ability to keep changing each time its 13 elements are placed together due to the quality of thread and cloth.'

The vulnerability of the works in this series is emphasized not only by the materials used, but also by stitch and construction. The loose, tentative stitches are insecure and threads are uncontrolled, suggesting broken lines of communication. Different elements can be easily reordered and changed; nothing is permanent.

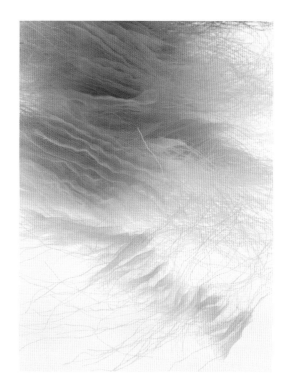

Opposite: Experimenting with tent stitch, dot stitch, cross stitch and variations on herringbone stitches, on lightweight cotton and silk fabrics.
Right: **12/13ths Asleep** *by Amanda Clayton.*

Shadow play

Dappled leafy shadows flickering across walls and floors convey a peaceful mood of tranquility. I was inspired by these qualities when I first began trying to capture shadows in my artwork. My practice at that time had started to explore the rural landscape around my home through walking and documenting what I experienced. One sunny day I found a long-forgotten pack of sun-print paper in my box of art materials and took it with me when I went out walking. Pausing in a clearing in the woods, I stooped to pick up whatever small natural objects I could find and made a print from them, there and then. The act of making a totally one-off print, out in the open air with barely any equipment, was inspiring. I was immediately hooked.

CYANOTYPE

Cyanotype, or blueprint as it is also known, is a photographic print process, distinctive for its striking Prussian blue colour. This is the same process that was used until the mid-20th century for architectural blueprints. It was invented in 1842 by the English astronomer Sir John Herschel, in his search for an effective way to reproduce his scientific notes and diagrams. *Photographs of British Algae: Cyanotype Impressions* by Anna Atkins, published in 1843, was arguably the first photographic book. The plates faithfully reproduce the botanical specimens not only with scientific accuracy, but also with an incredible beauty that has stood the test of time.

Blueprints are created by coating a porous surface (such as paper or fabric) with a solution of light-sensitive chemicals. A stencil or positive image is placed on top of the coated material to selectively block the light, and it is then exposed to UV (ultraviolet) light, i.e. sunlight. Once exposed, the work is removed from daylight, the stencil removed and the excess chemicals washed away in water to reveal the finished (negative) blue-and-white print. Areas that were covered by the stencil will appear white where the light was blocked and the chemicals not exposed. The remaining areas will be blue where the chemicals were able to react with sunlight. It is a satisfyingly simple method of creating a beautifully detailed print, and one that requires very little specialist equipment.

It is perhaps worth pointing out that cyanotype is not a dye process, nor does it have anything to do with indigo. The stunning blue colour and the ease with which it can be applied to textiles seems to give rise to some confusion in this regard.

Opposite: This large cyanotype print on cotton was made in a clearing in the woods using a few bracken stems. For me it captures a moment in time and place.

STENCILS

Unlike traditional darkroom photography, cyanotype prints are not created using an enlarger to project an image, but instead the stencil or object (positive) must be placed in direct contact with the light-sensitive material. Many people start with natural objects found readily to hand: leaves, grasses, seed heads, ferns and feathers all make excellent subjects. I particularly enjoy working with the most humble of weeds, collected from the pavements and old stone walls around my studio. The delicacy of herb robert, speedwell, common vetch and ivy-leaved toadflax create sensitive prints, picking up surprising details that would otherwise go unnoticed. It can be a wonderful way of seeing the world immediately around you in a whole new light. Other good shadow-making objects include lace and other transparent or mesh fabrics; fibres, string and trims; wire, old jewellery and buttons. Paper cut-outs and stencils can be used to create very reliable prints, but I admit to finding them rather dull. I aim to choose objects for their ability to tell a story or capture a moment.

Below: Prints can be made using a variety of stencils including plants, feathers and lace.

When choosing a subject to use as a stencil, look for its outline shape and notice any interesting details, such as holes or fibres. Hold it up to the light to get an idea of how it looks in silhouette. Sometimes an object can seem to be a really wonderful prospect, but when you look at the outline shape, you realize it will just print as a rather uninteresting blob. Experiment and explore the possibilities. I am frequently surprised by what can be achieved.

EQUIPMENT AND WORKSPACE

You will need

- Digital scales (must be capable of measuring small quantities – those sold for weighing jewellery are ideal)
- Measuring jug
- Clean jam jar
- Teaspoon or similar for dry chemicals
- Wooden or plastic spoon for stirring chemicals
- Wide paintbrush
- Washing-up bowl or bucket
- Glass clip frame (consisting of a backing board, a piece of glass and some metal clips that hold it all together)
- Apron or old clothes
- Surgical-style gloves
- Dust mask (only needed when handling the dry chemicals)
- For materials required for the light-sensitive chemical recipe, see page 56

A selection of brushes is useful to create different effects.

Preparing your workspace

Before starting work, prepare your workspace by shutting out daylight as much as possible. You do not need full darkroom conditions, you just need to eliminate as much UV light as you can. I have blackout blinds in my studio, which keep out enough of the daylight. But there is no need to stumble about in the dark, as normal household lamps and lighting pose no immediate risks to blueprinting. Cover surfaces with newspaper and/or plastic to protect them and to prevent contamination.

CYANOTYPE METHOD

Working safely

When using cyanotype, it is important to follow safe working practices to avoid harming yourself or others. Remember to ensure that none of your blueprint kit is ever used for food preparation.

- Never work in your kitchen or food preparation area.
- Do not use kitchen equipment for mixing or storing chemicals.
- Store dry chemicals and solutions in clearly labelled containers in a completely dark, dry place, out of the reach of children.
- Wear rubber (or similar) gloves.
- When working with powdered chemicals, avoid inhalation.
- Avoid contact with the skin and eyes.
- If chemicals get on the skin or into eyes, rinse immediately with water.
- Always wash your hands after using chemicals.
- Never pour waste chemicals into rivers or streams.

IMPORTANT: Never mix potassium ferricyanide with strong acids such as hydrochloric acid as this can create a chemical reaction resulting in toxic cyanide gas.

Prepare the light-sensitive chemical recipe

Working away from natural daylight (UV light), prepare the following recipe using the ingredients listed below:

- 30g ferric ammonium citrate (green)
- 15g potassium ferricyanide
- 250ml warm water

Measure the dry chemicals. Mix with the water, stirring until completely dissolved. The solution will be a bright lime green colour at this stage. The mixed chemical solution always works best when used as fresh as possible, so for best results, don't mix huge amounts if you don't plan to use it all. However, if you do find you have some left over, it can be successfully stored in a glass jar for over a month if kept in *complete* darkness. Be sure to keep it out of the reach of children and always label the contents clearly.

Application

In your prepared workspace, paint the cyanotype solution onto your chosen paper or textile backgrounds. Apply enough chemical to coat the paper or textile backgrounds but not so much that it pools on the surface. Allow to dry in a dark place, away from direct heat. Once coated, store them in the dark and use as soon as possible.

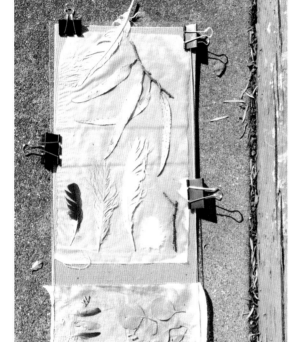

Exposing a print

Place one of the dried materials, coated side up, on the board part of the clip frame. Position the stencil objects. Place the glass on top and clip it in place to create a close contact. Take your work outside into bright sunlight. When the blueprint has exposed sufficiently, it will change colour to a greyish tone, and, depending on how strong the sunlight is, this can take between 5 and 20 minutes or more. Carry out some timed prints to establish how long is needed in your light conditions. Bear in mind that the UV light level will vary during the day and with the seasons.

While flat things make convenient stencils because they fit into a clip frame and create a good contact, there is no reason why you can't explore using three-dimensional objects, too. If working with three-dimensional objects, try pinning your prepared light-sensitive materials onto recycled polystyrene packaging or a cork board, then place or pin objects on top for exposure.

Wash out

Finish developing the print by immersing it in a bucket of water and washing it until the water runs completely clear and the white parts of the print show no signs of a green tinge. When washing textiles, squeeze the fabrics to ensure that all of the waste chemicals are washed out, but papers must just be lightly agitated without rubbing at the surface, as this can damage the print.

Hang textile prints to dry on a plastic washing line or clothes airer. Dry printed papers flat on newspaper.

Clean all utensils thoroughly in water after use. Wipe your washing line or clothes airer to avoid staining other items. Waste water can be safely poured down the drain and flushed with plenty of fresh water.

DIGITAL NEGATIVES

As an alternative to working with objects as a stencil, you can create your own photographic negative by printing a high-contrast black-and-white image onto an acetate sheet (make sure you buy the correct kind for your printer). Remember that the dark areas of the photo will appear white in the final print while the white or light areas will be blue, and if you want to invert your image, you can use photo-editing software.

In *Baptism*, I created a triptych of large cyanotype prints on silk habotai. The images of head, hands and feet were created with large-format digital negatives printed for me by a local print company. I also used real seaweed (dried and pressed in a flower press) as a stencil, to add more depth and detail.

Right: One of the digital negatives used to create **Baptism**.

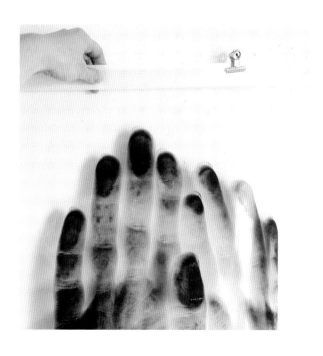

Opposite and left: **Baptism** *(2014). Cyanotype, hand stitch, appliqué, metal thread, silk, cotton. Each panel 73 x 90cm (29¾ x 35½in).*

OUT AND ABOUT

One of my favourite things about cyanotype printing is how spontaneous it can be. Once you have got to grips with the technique, it is quite easy to pack a lightproof bag with a bundle of pre-coated materials and head out into the countryside on a sunny day. I still love to make prints out in the fresh air, printing with whatever I find on my way. There is something quite exhilarating about being at the mercy of the elements; you never know what you might find or if the wind might just pick everything up and move it around for you.

Below: Dandelion clocks make for an ephemeral subject when printed out in the open air. Without glass it can be difficult to achieve a close enough contact for a clear print, but I enjoy experimenting to create lively, naturalistic prints.

CARING FOR BLUEPRINTED TEXTILES

While cyanotype prints are generally stable and long-lasting, there are some important issues to be aware of if you intend to wash your printed fabric. Alkaline substances, which will bleach the blue colour out of your print, are found in many washing detergents. Avoid laundry products containing chlorine bleach, ammonium hydroxide, tri-sodium phosphate, washing soda and baking soda. Some liquid laundry detergents for delicate handwashing are suitable, but always test on a sample first. Use water of a suitable temperature for your fabric.

Cyanotype prints can be ironed, but ironing on the reverse is recommended as excessive abrasion will damage your print. Again, use a suitable temperature for your fabric.

Left: Cyanotype print of eucalyptus on cotton.

Part Four
Fragment

Imperfect

In traditional needlework the pursuit of perfection was everything: the smallest of stitches, the straightest hem, the whitest linen; but today, in textile art, we have greater freedom of expression. While I greatly admire and respect the work of my great-grandmother, who stitched household linens with great care and skill, in my artwork I aim to capture something more organic, expressing something of the beautiful imperfections I see in the world. Weathered and worn surfaces, stained and marked cloth, things fractured, fragmented and mended, delicate, ethereal and fragile materials – all suggest to me the transience of life and the passage of time. Marked and aged textiles carry traces of intimate, personal histories in the stains and abrasions of wear and tear. Drawn to the poetic qualities of fragile, careworn textiles, I am mindful that ragged and stained materials can also be read as part of a narrative of poverty, neglect or despair. It is important to be aware of the different meanings old textiles can convey and how people may 'read' different things from a cloth.

Above: Weathered surface, peeling paintwork.

WABI-SABI

'Nothing lasts, nothing is finished and nothing is perfect.'[3]

Wabi-sabi is a Japanese term which we often hear used to describe objects with a shabby, rough or worn appearance. As an expression it is difficult to define in the English language because it sits within an entirely different cultural and world view. Connected to Zen Buddhism, wabi-sabi is an acceptance that the world is in a constant state of flux, of things coming into being and of fading and dying. Wabi-sabi principles are about accepting a simpler, perhaps more solitary life, uncluttered by many possessions. Most importantly it is about observing and taking delight in modest, quiet things and an awareness of impermanence in nature.

Objects that have a worn, imperfect, rough or unconventional appearance embody the spirit of wabi-sabi and are revered in traditional Japanese culture. Some material characteristics of wabi-sabi objects include:

- Raw or unfinished materials.
- Simple or rough forms.
- Humble or natural materials.
- Weathered or worn materials that have developed patina over time.
- Delicate objects and materials that suggest intimacy and fragility.
- Carefully mended objects.

Influenced by the principles of wabi-sabi since I first read about the subject as a student, I have always favoured asymmetrical shapes and forms, worn materials and things that show age marks or signs of construction. Although I wouldn't describe myself as a wabi-sabi practitioner, the principles and ideas influence my practice, helping me to consider my work within a much broader context of time and place, making and mindfulness.

Above: A delicate leaf skeleton.
Top: Antique patchwork fragments, stabilized with darning stitches.

[3]Richard R. Powell, *Wabi-sabi Simple* (Adams Media, 2004).

BALANCING CARE WITH CHAOS

When I work with aged materials or use a material in its raw state, it is important for me that it is done with intention. Wabi-sabi is never careless or reckless. It may appear effortless or organic, but it should always be carefully and skilfully made. I never make something crooked unless I want a more organic line. If my stitches vary in length, it is because I want them to do so. I always aim to balance care and attention to detail with an openness to things evolving and changing as the work progresses.

When working on a project I find myself trying to find a balance between executing my intended vision and allowing things to evolve organically. As I recently heard acclaimed artist Lubaina Hamid say, 'Always have a plan; but you don't necessarily have to stick to it.' Fundamentally I look to create something that is authentic and fulfils my intentions. My ideas might change but the initial feel that I want to communicate will still be there. As the work evolves I will ask myself: is this an honest, authentic response? Am I using techniques and materials with intention and integrity? Over time I have found that this internal dialogue has become integral to my working processes, and that decisions have become more intuitive. What follows are a few personal thoughts about choices I make with materials and making, which might help you find your own balance between perfection and imperfection.

FRAYED EDGES AND STRAY THREADS

When finishing a piece of work there are decisions to be made about loose threads and frayed edges. For me, there are no hard and fast rules. The most important thing is to go back to the starting point and consider what purpose the loose threads or raw edges serve in the work. Do they make the work appear unfinished, unresolved, raw, natural? Is that what you were striving for? If so, leave them as they are. On the other hand, if the threads obscure the work or convey the wrong message, tidy them up. I think it is important to consider whether loose threads and raw edges look intentional or not: do they look like part of the work, or as if you just couldn't be bothered to finish things properly?

FRONT OR BACK?

Why is it that the back of a piece of embroidery sometimes seems more appealing than the front? Could it be that the back of the work, created without overthinking, is more authentic, more intuitive? I often turn my work over while I am stitching to see what the effect is on the reverse. If

Above: Uneven stitches and loose threads are used here to represent handwritten notes from archival records.

I like what I see I might deliberately work from the 'wrong' side, so that the effect I like best ends up on the right side of the piece. I also like to consider the possibilities of double-sided or reversible pieces, or exploiting the three-dimensional possibilities of stitch on transparent fabrics (see page 46).

THE WORK IN PROGRESS

Remaining open to new possibilities is important in my working practice, observing and noticing things as I create that I didn't expect. Aim to work with an open and enquiring mind, remembering to pause and reflect during the process. In Part Five, I show examples where my work changed direction, where I saw the potential for alternative forms and formats by cutting up work in progress and reconfiguring it dramatically. Deciding when something is 'finished' is one of the hardest things in art. I once heard it referred to as 'cooking time', and that seems a fitting phrase. One of the core ideas of wabi-sabi is that everything is in a constant state of flux. Be open to the possibility that your artwork may never be truly 'finished' and that it is instead an ongoing expression of your practice and ideas at a given time.

Threadbare

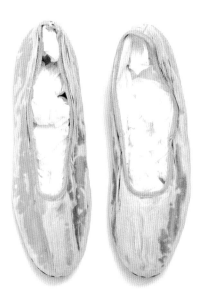

Threadbare textiles tell their own story of age and use. Tell-tale signs of damage, either through wear and tear or from the effects of age or climate, allude to their history of use and abuse. The main threats to textiles, in conservation terms, include damage from light or heat, which causes fading and makes fibres brittle; damp and humidity, causing mould damage or water staining; and pests, such as clothes moths, which like to devour the fibres themselves. Of course these threats can be a serious problem in terms of preserving precious historical textile objects, but at the same time I have always been drawn to old fabrics that have started to fade and disintegrate. One of the distinctive qualities of cloth is the way it wears out and breaks down; the fragility of

gently deteriorating cloth seems to make it even more precious and worthy of preserving.

As a little girl, I was enchanted by a pair of tiny porcelain dolls kept in a Victorian box in the top of my mother's wardrobe. The dolls were originally dressed in matching homemade silk dresses in a lovely shade of eau de nil, made by my grandmother, or perhaps her mother, but by the time I knew the dolls, their dresses were already in fragile tatters. Known as 'silk shattering', the problem is caused by the concentration of heavy metals commonly used in the 'weighting' of silk fabrics during the 19th and early 20th centuries. One of the good things about a worn or torn textile is that it often allows us to study its construction with greater ease, as is the case with the tiny silk dance shoes pictured above, where the surface of the satin fabric has disintegrated in areas, leaving just the stronger cotton warp threads remaining. Once damaged, secret layers of construction are revealed. The fragility of silk fibres can also be seen in the embroidery shown right, where the surface has disappeared to reveal a foundation of coarse linen.

BURNOUT

My interest in deconstructed surfaces led me to explore the fascinating process of devoré. Devoré, or burnout as it is sometimes known, is a print process applied to mixed-fibre textiles to selectively corrode one fibre, leaving the other undamaged. The devoré chemical paste is applied to the fabric and then baked to make the cellulose fibres brittle. The fabric is then washed to remove the chemically burned fibres. Often used on satin and velvet, where the resulting change in surface texture or transparency is most pronounced, the process can be used on any fabric that includes a mix of cellulose (plant) fibres with either protein or synthetic (often polyester) fibres, with a wide variety of results (see Different Effects, page 72, for more details).

This deconstructed textile, when used in an art context, communicates something fragile and ethereal or perhaps even haunting. Suspended in the process of disintegration, devoré fabrics give the impression of age and of organic matter withering, crumbling and decaying.

Below left: 17th-century Italian embroidery. The damaged and disintegrated silk embroidery reveals the layers of construction beneath.
Below: **The Sampling Project** *(2018). Detail. Several layers of printed, dyed and heavily devoréd fabrics.*

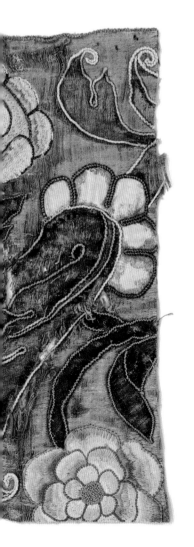

DEVORÉ TECHNIQUE

Materials

For this method I have focused on devoré that will burn cellulose fibres only. This means that your fabric will need to include a cellulose fibre and a fibre that is *not* cellulose, for example mixes of silk and viscose, polyester and cotton or bamboo and silk. Specialist suppliers sell fabrics specifically for devoré, but you can experiment with other mixed-fibre fabrics or pure cellulose fabrics. Use the burn test to check for fibre composition (see page 120).

You will need

- Devoré paste (see page 122)
- Masking tape
- Repositionable spray fabric glue (such as 505 Spray and Fix) (optional)
- Paintbrush (a stencil brush is useful, but any brush will work)
- Stencils (see below)
- Apron or old clothes
- Disposable plastic or surgical gloves
- Electric iron (a flat iron is best, but a steam iron with the steam turned off will also work)
- Heatproof surface or ironing pad

Stencils

For the most consistent professional results, devoré is printed through a silk screen prepared with a design. For simplicity at home, you can apply the paste freehand with a paintbrush or by printing through a stencil. You can design your own stencil from paper or stencil card, or experiment with 'found' stencils like leaves, or try paper doilies, henna dye stencils or other shop-bought stencils.

Working safely

When using any chemical, it is important to follow safe working practices to avoid harming yourself or others.
- Never eat or drink while you are working.
- Never work in your kitchen or food preparation area.
- Wear disposable plastic or surgical gloves.

Left: A set of old metal stencils were used to print this devoré sample on 100 per cent cotton fabric, leaving holes right through the cloth.

- Always wash your hands after using chemicals.
- Protect surfaces with newspaper and/or plastic and clean up afterwards.
- Clean all brushes, containers and tools after use and do not use for food storage or preparation.

Method

1. Use masking tape to secure the fabric to your covered work surface. If you are using a stencil, apply repositionable spray fabric glue on the back of the stencil and position it on the fabric.

2. Carefully apply devoré paste with a brush, using a stippling action, to the areas that you wish to burn out. Apply enough paste to penetrate the fibres sufficiently (it must not just sit on the surface), but try to avoid the paste seeping under the edges of the stencil. Move the stencil if you choose to, to apply further motifs, taking care not to smudge the printed areas.

3. Once you are happy with your design, allow the fabric to dry completely.

4. Remove all tape and stencils. Place the fabric on a heatproof surface or ironing pad. Using a medium iron, move the iron over your fabric until the areas of devoré start to change colour slightly to a light buff. It is important to ensure you heat all areas of the fabric equally, otherwise you might get patchy results. Be careful not to scorch the fabric by holding the iron in one place for too long.

5. Hand wash the fabric in hot soapy water, rubbing the surface to remove the damaged fibres. (It is advisable to place a spatter guard or sieve over the plug hole to prevent the drain becoming blocked with fibres.) When you are satisfied that the loose fibres have all been removed, rinse the fabric and hang it up to dry.

Different effects

The devoré process can be used with a variety of fabrics and stencils to produce a vast range of different appearances. These can be categorized into three key effects:

Changing the surface Silk or synthetic in warp and weft and cellulose in either direction (e.g., with satin or velvet fabrics).

Floating threads Silk or synthetic in either warp or weft and cellulose in the other direction.

Complete holes in the fabric Pure cellulose fabrics.

Further ideas

- Experiment with machine embroidery before devoré printing as a way of introducing additional supporting stitches. Use non-cellulose thread (silk or polyester).
- Dye or print your fabric. It is better to do this after devoré printing as it is easier to gauge the burnout on an undyed fabric.

Left: Additional silk threads were stitched into this silk/cotton mix fabric before devoré printing.

THE SAMPLING PROJECT

On a visit to the Tissuthèque archive in Roubaix, France, I was shown an exquisite collection of katagami (Japanese dyeing stencils). Katagami are cut from fine mulberry paper and sometimes held together by silk threads. I was struck by their intricate patterns and delicate structures. In response I devised a number of textile investigations, using combinations of natural dyeing, mordanting, devoré and stitching to develop my technical knowledge and to explore the visual and tactile qualities of the stencils. As a finished artwork *The Sampling Project* is presented as a series of textile samples, displayed to suggest archival processes, but also highlighting transparent, shadowy, lace-like effects.

Above and below: **The Sampling Project** *(2018).*

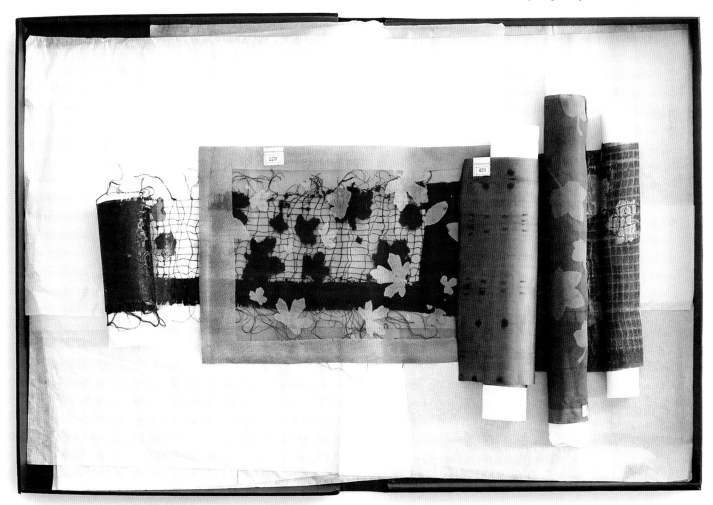

Lucy Brown

The importance of deconstructed material is immediately evident in the work of artist Lucy Brown. Sourcing second-hand clothing as the basis for much of her work. She says, 'For me cloth is, clothes are, part of the essence of our lives. I grew up in a family environment where cloth, clothes, materials and making skills were things to value and be in awe of, physically, emotionally and psychologically. My selected materials have to have a connection with my ideas and thinking, otherwise the work does not happen. The wearing and trying on of the garment raw materials is a way of me getting a physical connection with the materials, maybe trying to make them mine? But it is important to keep the garments' integrity within the work.'

The embodied memory held invisibly within the fibres of the sourced garments is deconstructed through cutting, unpicking and ripping. This deconstructed cloth takes on new form in woven installation works and anti-form sculptures. Lucy's artwork *the secrets we keep from ourselves...* was developed and made in response to research into Nottingham's heritage of lace manufacturing. The warp threads of Nottingham Leavers lace are interwoven with sections of women's clothing, to deconstruct and reconstruct the lives of women mill workers.

In Lucy's *Offerings* series, the private and public role of cloth and clothing is made apparent, through her working process – partly made in her private studio and completed in the public realm of the gallery. The intimate private/public making and the choice of materials reference the female body. Describing one of the pieces, she says, '*Waisted/wasted* reworks areas of the waist and hips into silver grey ribbons, pinned and re-(loomed) tensioned, cutting through the architecture of the gallery space ... bringing herself to you.'

Left: **Waisted/wasted** *(2018) by Lucy Brown. Woven anti-form sculpture. Ribbon and deconstructed garments.*

74

Below: **the secrets we keep from ourselves ...** *by Lucy Brown. Woven, anti-form installation. Lace, trims and deconstructed garments. Detail shown left.*

Cobweb

First developed in the late 19th century, 'chemical lace' or guipure was originally a process for creating imitation lace by machine-embroidering cotton threads onto a fine silk fabric, which was then immersed in a corrosive bath of chemicals to dissolve the silk. It seems incredible that such a delicate material could be produced from such a destructive process, yet the very idea of a disappearing cloth seems like magic.

Modern soluble fabrics have since been developed that can simply be dissolved in water, as a method of creating light, open fabrics from machine embroidery. The delicacy of this machine-made 'lace' can be used to create transparency in an artwork; the intricate network, supported only by the connecting stitches, evokes a sense of vulnerability, frailty or impermanence. A great variety of effects can be achieved by varying the threads used and the density or style of stitching.

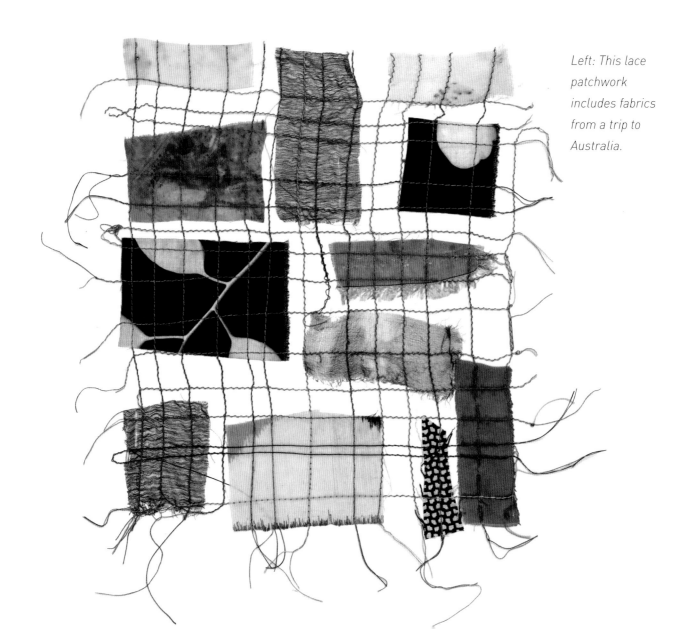

Left: This lace patchwork includes fabrics from a trip to Australia.

DISAPPEARING MATERIALS

A range of dissolvable fabrics are available, including hot- or cold-water soluble fabrics, as well as woven materials that work in a similar fashion to devoré and are scorched with an iron to remove fibres. I find the most useful of these products is cold-water soluble fabric. I normally choose the thicker, non-woven dissolvable fabrics that feel more like interlining, rather than the transparent film-like versions, which are rather prone to splitting. You can also buy soluble fabrics that are tacky (to hold materials in place), which are worth experimenting with for the lace patchwork technique.

LACE PATCHWORK

While traditional guipure lace effects are created simply with stitches, there are a wide variety of alternative techniques. One approach is to create a lacy patchwork by working with small fragments of material, joining them together into a new fabric.

Piecing together scraps of different materials on a theme is an interesting way to develop a narrative through the meanings suggested by different textiles. Using this technique, prints, patterns and textures can be combined to create pieces imbued with personal meaning or narrative. Materials might relate to a particular person, place or time, or join together different parts of something to create a 'family' of pieces. Each piece could be different, using precious scraps of antique textile, or swatches from family clothing, or they could simply be snippets from the same textile, torn apart to indicate ideas around fracturing or separation. Depending upon the density of your stitches, the lattice of embroidery will emphasize and strengthen the connections between the textile fragments, or highlight how fragile those links are.

For my lace patchwork sample (shown left), I selected snippets of fabrics collected during a trip to Australia. There are scraps of cyanotype prints, vintage textiles and pieces of naturally dyed fabric that still smell of the eucalyptus they were dyed with.

LACE PATCHWORK TECHNIQUE

The method described sets out the basic process, but this can be adapted and developed with your own fabrics to create a personal narrative.

You will need

- Two pieces of cold-water soluble fabric a little larger than you want your finished fabric to be
- Small scraps or pieces of fabric of your choice
- Machine thread (the thread you use on both top *and* bottom [spool] threads will be visible in your work)
- Sewing machine

Method

1. Place your scraps onto a piece of soluble fabric, leaving gaps in between. The size of gap will determine how open or solid the final result is. Place the second piece of soluble fabric on top to sandwich the scraps, and pin to secure.

2. Machine stitch parallel lines of straight stitch across your fabric sandwich, making sure you stitch across all of the fabric scraps. Turn the work and make rows of stitches perpendicular to the first set of lines, creating a stitched grid.

3. Hold the work up to the light to check your stitching lines. Anything that is not linked with stitching will fall apart when the soluble fabric is washed away.

4. Carefully wash the work under running water, making sure you wash away any stickiness from the soluble fabric. Leave to dry. If you want the work to be soft, ensure you wash the work very thoroughly. If after drying your work is still stiff you can rewash it to remove any further residue.

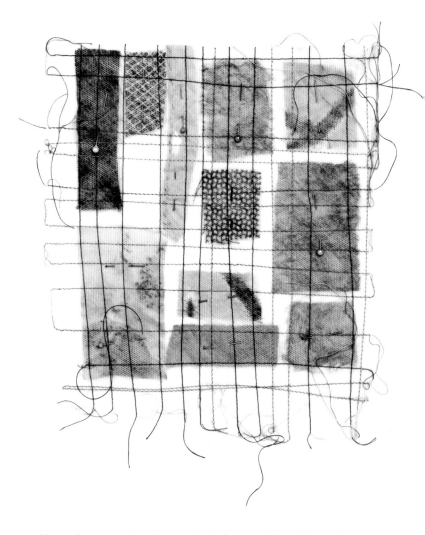

Above: Lace patchwork sample before washing. Ensure the lines of stitching cross through all your fabric pieces.

When working on particularly delicate pieces, it can be useful to stretch and pin your work on a piece of cork board or polystyrene foam to help it keep its shape and avoid it tangling during washing. You can then leave it on the board to dry flat.

Further ideas

- Experiment with fragments of patterned or printed fabric collected together to suggest a narrative. You could even print your own images onto cloth.
- Explore a variety of different sewing threads, or mix different colours for the top and bottom threads of your sewing machine.
- Working free-motion embroidery will give you more freedom with the pattern of stitches. For this you will need a darning foot, embroidery hoop and lowered feed dog.

Above: Simple leaf shapes cut from vintage fabrics were joined together with machine stitch in this sample.

Cecilia Heffer

Describing her intensive machine-stitching process as 'a form of walking', Cecilia Heffer uses repetitive thread structures as a way of drawing together complex narratives. She describes her pieces as 'lace works', situating them within contemporary lace practice, and says, 'the making of a textile for me is a creative response to the transient nature of the places we work and live in'.

The *Lace Narratives* series is a collection of 'intimate textile paragraphs that make up a collective story of migration'. Each work embodies fragmented memories between two cultures: Chile and Australia. The series is a direct response to Cecilia's own family heritage, having moved to Australia from Chile with her family as a young child. Cecilia sees the pattern of holes and gaps in her work as being as important as the solid areas. In *Lace Narratives* the composition of elements highlights the disjointed and imperfect nature of family memory and narrative: 'They are designed to be read as small lace postcards and are intended to provoke a fragmented story of place.' The works incorporate pictorial and abstract elements, assembled from parts made up of antique laces, handkerchiefs, official passports, letters and natural dye samples.

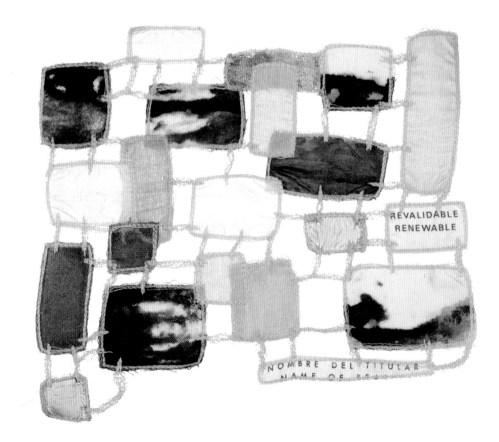

Right: **Reimagined Landscapes** *(2010) by Cecilia Heffer. Cotton, linen, silk, natural eucalyptus dyes, iron mordant handkerchief, photographic transfer and stitching onto soluble substrate. 17 x 15cm (6½ x 6in).*

Right: **Lace Passport**
(2010) by Cecilia Heffer.

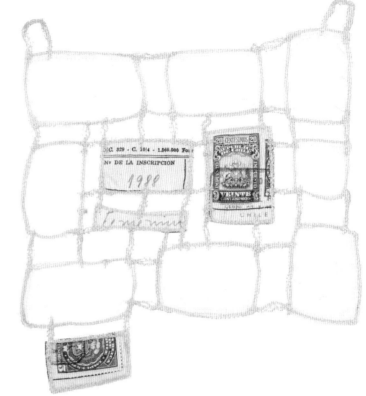

Below: **Lace Passport**
(2010) by Cecilia Heffer.

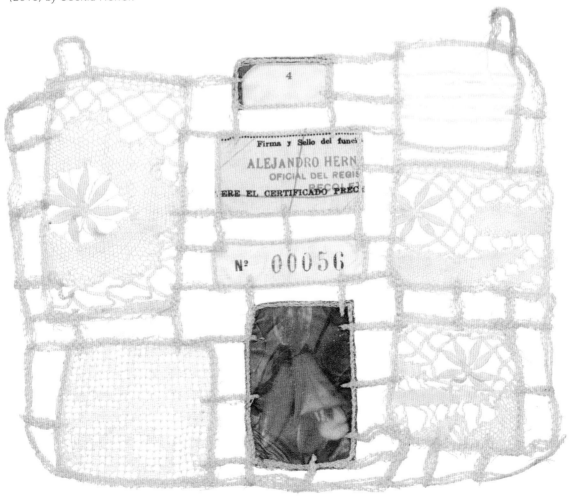

Part Five
Mend

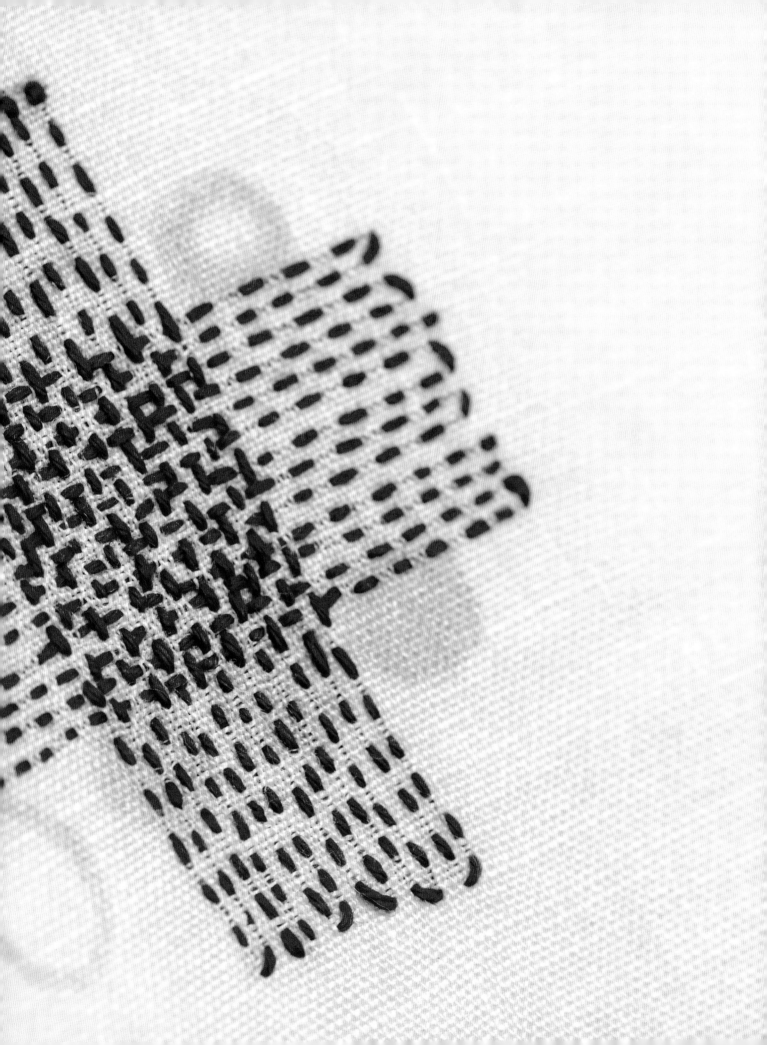

Patch

Traditionally mending was an act of thrift, when resources needed to be carefully managed. Carefully patching a worn or torn garment would have extended its life by stabilizing and reinforcing the weak area. Until relatively recently even very wealthy households would darn or patch household linens and undergarments because cloth and clothing was expensive. However, it was seen as important to make those mends as invisible as possible in order to avoid drawing attention. Patches and mends were seen as a sign of poverty, and therefore something to be ashamed of. I have always been drawn to old textile items that have been sensitively mended and patched because they show that an item has been cared for and valued. For artist Louise Bourgeois, the act of stitching and mending was used as a metaphor for her art and life; creation, destruction and reparation were central themes explored through material and making:

'When I was growing up, all the women in my house were using needles. I've always had a fascination with the needle, the magic power of the needle. The needle is used to repair the damage. Its claim to forgiveness. It is never aggressive, it's not a pin.'[4]

Perhaps this thoughtful act of reparation can hold deeper meaning. Breaking and remaking can certainly help us to feel more connected to our materials, by becoming a part of the construction process.

Right: **Spring Oriental Vase** *(2015) by Zoë Hillyard. Ceramic, textile and hand stitch. 28 x 17cm (11 x 6¾in).*

---

[4] Louise Bourgeois, as cited in Robert Storr, *Intimate Geometries: The Art and Life of Louise Bourgeois* (Thames & Hudson, 2016).

Zoë Hillyard

Sitting outside traditional patching and piecing techniques, the 'ceramic patchwork' techniques of Zoë Hillyard nonetheless exploit very similar processes of breaking and remaking. Describing her pieces as 'stitch-reconstructions', the process begins with discarded and broken ceramic vessels. The shards are carefully covered in cloth that are then stitched together using a method of her own devising. This highly individual technique has been arrived at through extensive investigation. The appeal of her work comes not only from the visual surprise at the contrast of soft and hard materials being interchanged, but also from the mixing of patterns. She describes her practice as 'an ongoing battle between control and spontaneity'.

'During making, I become intimately involved in the subtle dynamics of the relationship of my chosen materials as I adapt my process to balance the tensions between stitch, textile and gravity. Shattering and chipping of ceramics during the early stages of the process, results in holes appearing within the final outcomes. These "imperfections" are often complemented by a deliberate partial rebuilding of the vessel. They are fundamental to the character of each piece and the focal point by which the viewer navigates round the three-dimensional form. My pieces are "softly solid", containing both strength and vulnerability and as such, are reminders of the transitory nature of life.'

Above: **Katharina's Bowl** *(2018) by Zoë Hillyard.*
Ceramic, textile and hand stitch. 13 x 27cm (5 x 10¾in).

PATCHING: A PERSONAL RELATIONSHIP TO CLOTH

Some of my own clothes have received the patching treatment over the years, including several pairs of well-worn jeans; by mending them with patches cut from other old jeans I have been able to extend their life. The more I add to the mending, the more my connection to the cloth grows; the time spent mending increases my emotional investment in the jeans.

Time spent handling and working with cloth gives us a deeper understanding of its properties and a more personal relationship to our materials. In my artwork I sometimes use patching as a way of mending a fragile or worn fabric, but more often to represent an interruption in a surface or to create detail. I like to add small patches onto a larger background cloth, breaking up a solid area in an artwork. An expensive silk, a rare fragment of vintage cloth, or a patterned fabric draws the eye as an accent. Using only a very small amount of a richly patterned or detailed fabric seems to have the effect of elevating it to something precious, whereas if used in any quantity the cloth would have been gaudy or overwhelming. Used like this, a patch becomes more akin to the embroidered decorative patches used as a feature on clothing. The patch becomes an emblem, a token or souvenir.

I use different ways to stitch a patch depending on the weight of the cloth and the effect I am looking for.

Above: **In Search of Green** *(2013). Detail of installation. The patches on this small garment hold the piece together but also add detail and patches of colour.*

RUNNING REPAIRS: A VERY QUICK PATCH

At its most basic a patch is a piece of cloth stitched over a hole or weak area. If you simply want a small section of another fabric introduced into the work you can cut a piece and sew it on, without turning under the edges, with a simple running stitch or blanket stitch or oversew it. This works well for heavyweight fabrics that might be difficult to hem, or if you want to see the raw edges of the fabric.

Above: A simple running stitch holds the most basic form of patch in place.

A TRADITIONAL HEMMED PATCH

This is the traditional method of patching, which would normally be made as inconspicuous as possible, using matching fabric and thread. You may wish to use contrasting colours or patterns to make your patch visible, but I suggest working with a similar weight of fabric so that the patch sits well on the cloth.

Method

If working with a badly damaged fabric with a big hole, you may find it useful to tack it onto a piece of scrap paper to provide support. I find it sometimes helps to stretch the fabric taut before adding the patch.

1. Cut the patch fabric slightly larger than the finished patch needs to be, creating an allowance for hemming. Turn under the edges of the patch and pin or tack in place on the right side of the fabric, covering the hole or damaged area entirely.
2. Hand stitch around the edge of the patch using very small diagonal hem stitches. Alternatively, use 'slip hemming' – catching the edge of both fabric and patch fabric and sliding the needle along inside the fold so that the stitches are almost invisible.

First tack the patch in place, then carefully fold under the edge and use slip hemming to hold it securely in place. The stitches should be almost invisible if done correctly.

3. On the wrong side of the fabric, cut away the damaged fabric into a neat square or rectangle, leaving enough fabric to hem. Snip into each corner, close to but not through the stitching. Fold under the raw edge of the square hole and carefully hand stitch the hem. No raw edges should be visible when finished. Ironing your work after stitching helps to settle the patch in its place.

Further ideas

- To create a patch that is less uniform, you don't have to cut straight edges. Sometimes I like to pin the patch in place and then fold under the hem as I stitch, which leads to a more organic-shaped patch.
- If the patch is purely decorative (rather than mending an actual hole), you can place it wherever you like. Use the same technique as for a traditional hemmed patch, but choose whether to cut and stitch the reverse of the patch or just create an appliqué swatch on the front.

Below left: The patch from the reverse side. Below: For this sample I selected a scrap of printed fabric to create a contrast.

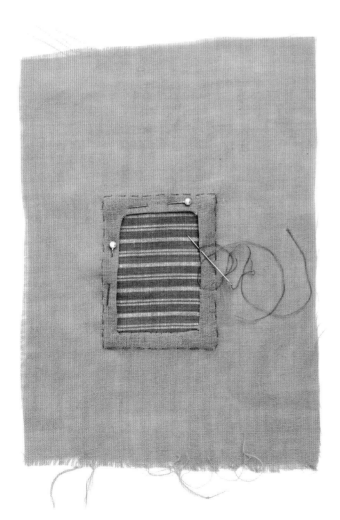

Seam

I have always been drawn to traditions of patching and piecing, a kind of 'making good' with materials, using up the leftover bits, remnants or portions that remain when fabric becomes too worn. This in turn offers possibilities for joining together materials in different combinations, constructing new visual narratives. Each scrap of fabric adds something to the story. Gathering and joining materials has become a natural way for me to compose elements into a larger piece. Working with an existing palette of fabrics, cutting and piecing them together, allows me to play with composition and edit in a 'cut-and-paste' style, cropping in close to areas of interest.

When faced with a pile of beautiful fabrics carefully selected for a project, it can feel somewhat daunting to take the plunge with stitching, let alone cutting them up. A plan or system can be hugely helpful. Whilst it might sound contradictory to say that structure provides freedom, having some rules or guidelines mean there are fewer decisions to make, freeing you up to concentrate on the overall effect of your developing work.

We often think of improvisation as an entirely spontaneous and random act, but in fact it is all about creatively playing within parameters. When improvising, actors, musicians and comedians will seemingly invent new ideas in the moment, but they usually do this within or alongside an existing framework of limitations. In textile terms, there are a number of ways that we can introduce limits on piecing together fabrics and improvising with what you have can become a highly creative and inspiring process.

Opposite: Improvised patchwork in progress.

IMPROVISED FABRIC PIECING

Using a planned approach to exploring your fabrics can help you to build confidence as you learn how materials behave together in terms of colour, texture and structure. Start with a limited range of fabrics and colours as this helps to reduce the need for decision-making. Limit yourself to just three to begin with: a small amount of two and a larger amount of another that acts as your dominant or background colour. The technique described below will be easier with fabrics of a similar weight, but don't let that prevent you from experimenting.

2.

3.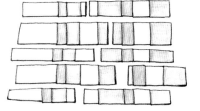

4.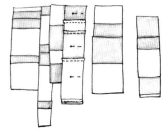

5.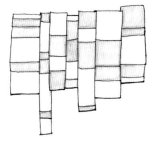

Method

1. Cut all three fabrics into strips of different widths, ranging in width from about 4cm (1½in) to 12cm (4¾in). Your strips should be at least 30cm (11¾in) long but there is no need to be too precise about measurements or straightness.

2. Seam the strips together using machine or hand stitching, joining them along the long edges with a seam allowance of about 1cm (½in). Try to avoid placing the same colour strips next to each other. Use up all of the pieces, forming one big piece of seamed cloth. Trim to level up the edges.

3. Now cut this new cloth into strips, cutting crossways through the existing strips and again cutting a range of widths between 5cm and 12cm (2in and 4¾in). Cut each strip into two shorter strips of varying lengths.

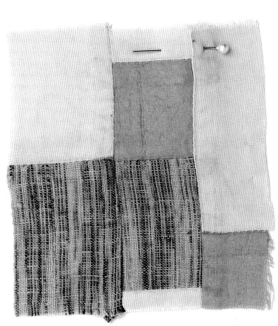

4. Next you will piece together the strips in a new configuration. Move and rearrange the strips, flipping and shuffling them until you settle on a pleasing arrangement. Aim to make your arrangement varied and random rather than looking to create a repetitive pattern. Once you are happy with the arrangement, stitch the strips together.

5. Stand back from your pieced fabric and review. It may be helpful to pin it on a wall or peg it onto your washing line. Another alternative is to hold it up in front of a mirror, which, oddly, can help to give you a more objective viewpoint. Reflect on the composition and balance of colour; are some areas more successful or pleasing to the eye? Try using strips of paper to mask off areas that are less successful. You can either think of it as one large piece or focus in on smaller areas to create a series of coordinating pieces. When you are happy, cut out the fabric sections that you want to keep (as above).

REVISING AND REVISITING WORK

Sometimes when creating a piece, I find things don't work out as I hoped. Perhaps it doesn't convey what I had in my mind's eye, or maybe it is visually flawed in some way. For me, accepting this and finding ways to move on with a project often means being bold and taking the scissors to my work. Take the time to review and reconfigure your pieces, selecting the bits that work and cropping out sections that don't, or seam in sections of additional cloth onto existing pieces.

Below: Compositions made from improvised patchwork of wool and paper were cut up, inked and turned into printing plates.

MATERIAL EVIDENCE

When I was invited to make work for an exhibition called Material Evidence at Sunny Bank Mills, I was fortunate to be given small samples of fine worsted suiting fabrics made when the mill was still a prominent textile manufacturer. Combining these fabrics with locally produced cream wool flannel, I created an improvised patchwork cloth, further embellished with embroidered lettering in red stitches. When completed, I reviewed the work and although I liked aspects of it, overall it didn't look quite right, so I took the bold decision to cut it up and explore a new direction. Cropping and cutting over a period of several days, I ended up with a series of much smaller panels, which I was much happier with. I chose to further subvert my original plan by using some of these sections as printing plates, creating a whole other dimension to the experimental possibilities of the cloth.

Two large transparent textile panels were also produced for this exhibition, using improvised patchwork techniques. *Bastard Cloth* I & II were made in response to the architecture of the mill, where internal windows and geometric structures seem to mirror the detailed woven fabrics held in the company's archives.

Below: **Bastard Cloth I & II** *(2015). Cotton, linen, paper and wool patchwork piecing with hand stitch and appliqué.*

Matthew Harris

Back and forth, making and unmaking, in his practice Matthew Harris uses a constant process of revision to generate his complex yet subtle compositions. He says, 'I am not interested in "perfect" textiles but rather in a cloth that is made imperfect as a result of tears, patches, darns and frayed edges. Held together with a utilitarian stitch, these random and chaotic interruptions in the pattern and surface of the cloth provide the impetus for my work.'

Often based on an initial drawing, he constructs his work from layers of cotton twill dustsheet marked with dye and pigment, which is pushed through the layers of cloth. The reworking and restructuring process investigates a 'strata of shape, mark and colour' that he excavates in order to reveal the image that he wants.

'The process by which I create and construct images through an alternating rhythm of paper and cloth, paint and dye, has become a ritual of making and unmaking, built up and laid down over many years. Working the material is at the heart of this ritual. Not just the physical material of paper, cloth, thread, etc., but the material stuff of an image.'

Through this process he moves fragments around, 'flipping cloth over, turning it around, inserting additional scraps, pinning and repinning until a final image emerges'. These final images, while successful in their own right, feel like something still in a state of flux; their patched and pieced construction feels somehow temporary, 'always with the potential for change, held at a still point, neither perfect nor finished'.

Right: **Cloud Tree Fragment**
by Matthew Harris.
36 x 46cm (14¼ x 18in).

Left: **Field Note Fragment** *by Matthew Harris. 26 x 25cm (10 x 9¾in)*

Left: **Field Note Fragment** *by Matthew Harris. 20 x 24cm (8 x 9½in).*

Darn

Fabrics that have been darned suggest a level of care that we seldom take with our everyday textiles and clothing now, similar in that respect to patching. But darning stitches can introduce wonderful texture and detail to textile art. Darning suggests a gentle manipulation of the structure of the cloth, drawing attention to how the artist has chosen to interact with it. At its most basic, the darning technique can be used as a subtle supporting layer with darning stitches providing scaffolding to delicate and fragile fabrics. Cobweb-thin silks and moth-eaten antique cloth can be underpinned with rows of running stitch. With the most fragile of these, a layer of backing fabric beneath will provide additional reinforcement.

Where traditional darning was always intended to be as discreet as possible, when used in an art context we can choose to draw attention to the stitches and their role in the construction of the work, especially where this is part of how we want the viewer to read the work. Visible stitches, perhaps in a contrasting colour, draw attention to the fragility of the material and the care taken to choose it. Alternatively, darning could be used simply to highlight the hand of the maker as a kind of signature. Contrasting darning stitches can also be used to explore narratives about emotional and physical care, damage and repair.

In *Visible Mending* (2013), I created a large linen tablecloth printed with a design enlarged from an original wartime military-issue embroidery kit that belonged to my grandmother, who served in the army during the Second World War. I stitched multiple darns in khaki wool into the pretty linen cloth as a reminder of my grandmother's brother, my great-uncle, who also served, but who was captured and spent much of the war imprisoned in a POW (prisoner-of-war) camp. Small silk patches have been printed with the newspaper cutting reporting him as 'missing in action', as well as the details of his POW number and address. My grandmother recollected that when he returned home after the war, her brother's official issue pullover was almost entirely made up of darns, his skill with a needle and thread having held him and his clothes together while he was incarcerated. Like so many people affected by war, he spoke little about his ordeal, but returned with invisible scars. Alongside the khaki darns there are darns of red crosses, representing the Red Cross parcels that sporadically reached him, as well as reminding us of the psychological wounds of war that often remain hidden from view.

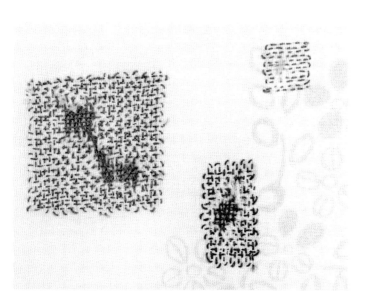

Left: **Visible Mending** *(2013). Detail.*

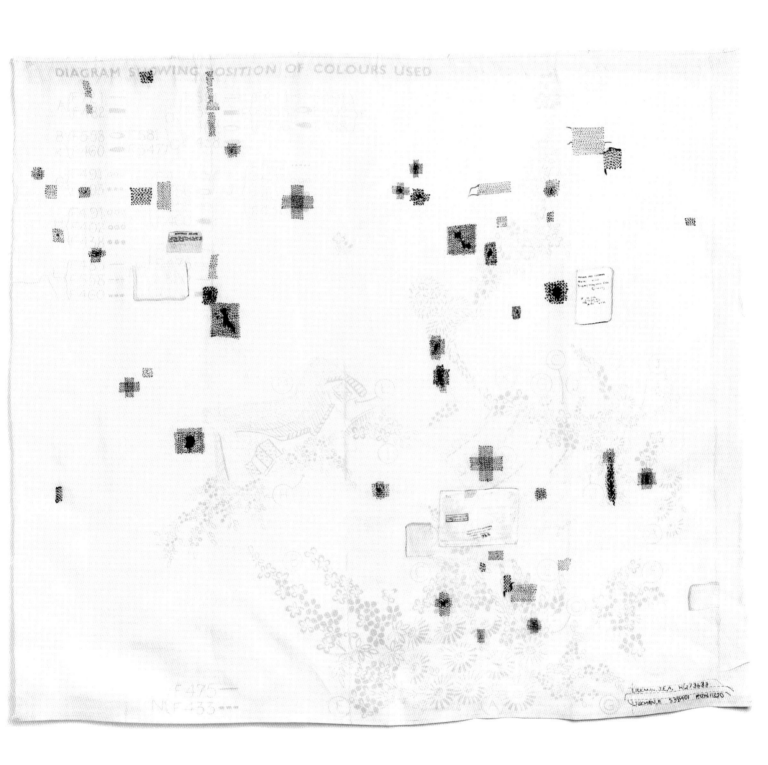

Above: **Visible Mending** *(2013). Digitally printed linen and silk with darning.*

SURFACE DARNING

An alternative method of darning, this technique can be used to create decorative stitches as an additional layer on top of the fabric. It provides a satisfying way of introducing small patches of intricately woven threads on top of an existing cloth.

Method

1. Stretch the base fabric taut in an embroidery frame or hoop. It is crucial that the work is kept tightly stretched. If the fabric relaxes, the stitches will pull and pucker the fabric.
2. Mark out the shape you wish to cover with surface darning, using a fabric chalk pencil or a disappearing pen or pencil.
3. Thread a needle with about 40cm (15¾in) of a smooth embroidery thread such as cotton a broder or perlé (stranded embroidery cottons are not appropriate as it is too difficult to distinguish between individual stitches).
4. Starting from one side of your marked shape, make a long stitch all the way across from one edge to the opposite side. Bring the needle back up close to where the previous stitch ended, leaving just a few fabric threads between each stitch, then stitch back to the opposite edge. Continue with these stitches until the whole shape is covered with long stitches all aligned next to each other: these are your warp stitches. Try to avoid long stitches on the back of the work; if you turn the work over, you should just see tiny stitches around the outside of the shape.

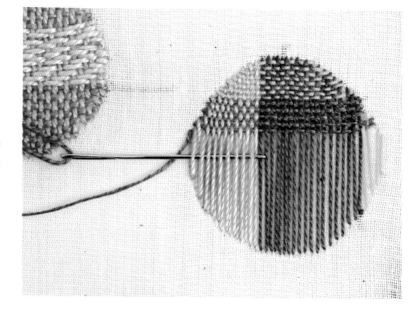

5. Select the thread you wish to use to stitch the weft stitches, in the other direction. This could be the same or different to your warp thread. Bring the needle up on the edge of the shape, ready to stitch perpendicular to the previous warp stitches. This time you will weave the new weft stitches in and out of alternating warp threads. To make this easier use either a blunt-ended tapestry needle or the blunt end of your needle, which will help you to avoid accidentally stitching through the previous stitches. When you have gone right across the shape, take the needle back through the fabric on the line.

6. Bring the needle back up next to the previous stitch and go back across, weaving in and out on alternate threads from the previous row. This requires a great deal of concentration, so take your time. Extra care taken with the first few rows of weaving will stand you in good stead, as it is difficult to recover the weaving once the alternating lines get out of step.

7. Continue stitching until the entire shape is woven. You may find it helpful to push each line of weaving down with the blunt end of the needle, to ensure the pattern is firm and compact.

Opposite and above: A collection of darns including simple reinforcement and surface darning with a variety of different threads and effects.

Further ideas

- When choosing your threads, experiment with different colours and textures (matte or shiny).
- Use different thread colours in bands to create a checked effect.
- Try different weave structures by going under one thread and over two to create a twill weave, which should look like diagonal lines once complete.
- For a less compact weave structure, leave bigger gaps between rows to create a looser, more organic appearance.

Lorna Muir

Photographs taken by Martin Parr of a remote farming community in West Yorkshire during the 1970s were the starting point for a collection of pieces by Lorna Muir. It is an area she is very well acquainted with, having lived and worked nearby. She says, 'My work reflects an intuitive and personal response to the natural and built environment and the lives of the inhabitants of that landscape. Fabrics, threads and stitches were selected for colour and texture to reflect the industrial heritage within the hills and valleys.' The pieces take the form of hats and coats, reflecting the contrast between shabby workday clothing and the garments kept smart for 'Sunday best'. In her work, 'stitches are used as a kind of poetry to convey an emotional and personal response'. The patched and darned materials used represent the endurance of cloth and body, the harsh landscape and a lifestyle that takes its toll on both.

Left: **Sarah Hannah Greenwood's Coat** *(2018) by Lorna Muir. Wool tweed, surface embroidery and appliqué in wool and cotton.*
Opposite: Darning sample (2018) by Lorna Muir. Hand stitch on wool cloth.

Part Six
Lustre

Patina

**patina: 1 the oxidized surface film on metal, esp. bronze or copper.
2 the sheen on a surface caused by handling.**

The build-up of surface patina on antique furniture is often seen as a valuable attribute. It recalls the years of use and the hands that have polished it; it speaks of authenticity, age and quality. Perhaps it is for these reasons that I am drawn to textiles that also bear the marks of use, and those that appear to have layers of material archaeology.

Patina is a word usually used to describe the softly reflected light on worn and weathered hard materials: brass, copper, pewter, wood, perhaps leather, too. While not usually associated with textiles, richly tactile and lustrous effects can be achieved on cloth by layering different surface treatments and finishes. When I first started experimenting with waxing materials I was inspired by the work of artist J. Morgan Puett, who used beeswax as a way of artfully preserving a collection of her artefacts, documents and fashion garments. The idea of using beeswax as a preservative made perfect sense to me, as I was then looking at ways of preserving memory in cloth, and in fact attempting to capture and retain the memory of special places, experiences and transient thoughts is behind many of the processes that I continue to work with today.

Inspired to explore my own method of applying wax to textiles, I discovered a very simple method that can be used to create diverse effects depending on the material coated. A coating of beeswax can give a warm, lustrous sheen to textile surfaces, making some fabrics, such as fine silks, slightly translucent. Wax can also be used to visually unite different surfaces. In *Fragments Patched* I created a small patchwork-inspired piece from naturally dyed silks and cyanotype printed card. By coating the pieces with beeswax, the colours have become richer, warmer, and all the elements seem to tie in with each other. The wax also has the effect of consolidating the different surfaces and the joins between, harmonizing the separate patches.

Left: **Fragments Patched II** *(2013). Paper, textile, wax, natural dyes, cyanotype, hand stitch. Approx. 20 x 20cm (8 x 8in).*

WAXING TEXTILES

You will need

- Pelleted beeswax (or soy wax if you prefer)
- Fabrics or papers of your choice (test small samples of materials to see which you like best before embarking on a large piece)
- Baking parchment
- Iron
- Heat-proof pad or old ironing board

Method

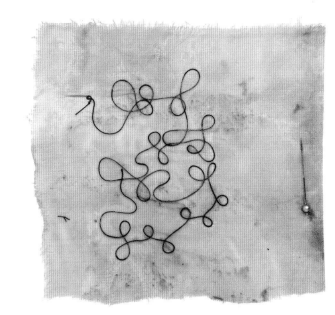

1. Cut two pieces of baking parchment larger than your fabric or paper pieces. Place one on your ironing surface, followed by the fabric/paper. Sprinkle beeswax pellets over the fabric/paper and cover with the second piece of baking parchment.
2. Run a hot iron over the baking parchment until the wax has melted and been absorbed into the fabric/paper. Be careful that melted wax does not seep out from the edges of the baking parchment, as it will be very hot.
3. Allow to cool completely. If you have areas where the wax has not penetrated, you can sprinkle on more wax pellets and repeat the process.

Above: A selection of waxed and stitched fabrics.

WAXING AND STITCH

Because wax has the ability to make some lightweight materials transparent, it can be interesting to explore how stitch interacts, stitching either before or after applying wax. Stitching made before waxing will be embedded into the wax and becomes part of the surface, whereas stitches added after will sit above the surface. Review the shadow stitch techniques on page 49 as a starting point.

Debbie Lyddon

The work of Debbie Lyddon is characterized by the slow transformation of cloth through processes that are relevant to the coastal locations that influence her work, as is apparent in her *Ground Cloths* series, as she describes: 'Inspired by sails and tarpaulins that are found everywhere on the coast, the *Ground Cloths* take the form of large sail "fragments". Rocks and earth gathered from local beaches are processed to colour the cloth and to create a subtle interpretation of place, material and object. Traditionally, sailors and fishermen would protect sails, ropes and nets by "dressing" them with a mixture of linseed oil, wax and red ochre to give protection from the elements. I have experimented with, and subtly altered, the traditional techniques of waterproofing and preserving cloth by substituting red ochre with locally collected materials – chalk, sea-coal and yellow ochre – to produce a blend that both protects and preserves the *Ground Cloths*.'

Above: **Ground Cloth: Chalk** *by Debbie Lyddon. Detail showing the build-up of surface patina created using chalk, oil, beeswax and seawater.*

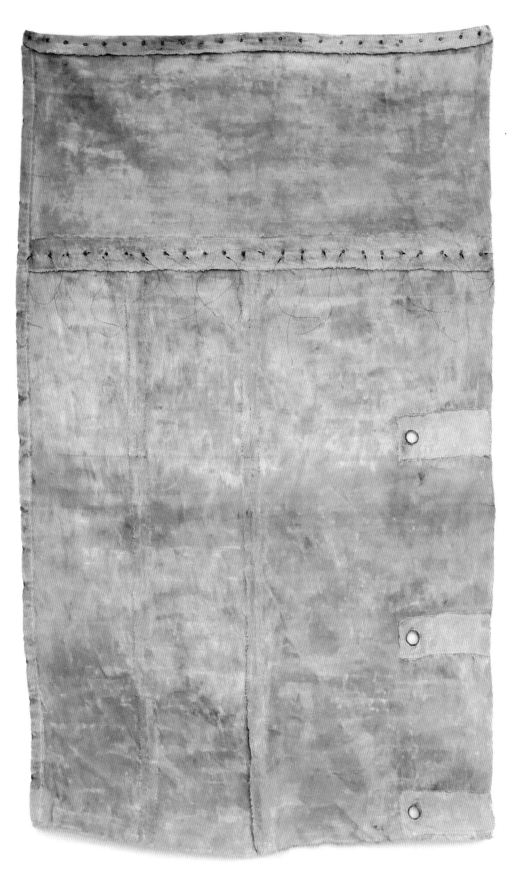

Left: **Ground Cloth:
Chalk** *by Debbie Lyddon.
Linen, wire, hand-
collected and hand-
ground chalk, linseed oil,
beeswax, seawater,
found threads.
120 x 197cm
(47¼ x 77½in).*

Diana Harrison

As part of a site-specific installation, responding to a disused area of Salts Mill, a former textile mill turned art gallery in Saltaire, West Yorkshire, for the Cloth & Memory {2} exhibition (2013), Diana Harrison chose to make a departure from her usual format of the quilt. Instead, her piece, *Handkerchiefs*, was created from a collection of vintage cotton handkerchiefs, repurposed and subjected to her distinctive process of dyeing and printing. The additive and subtractive processes of dyeing and bleaching out create a kind of

Above: **Handkerchiefs** *(2013) by Diana Harrison. Recycled cotton handkerchiefs, overdyed, bleached and hand-stitched together. Approx. 500cm x 250cm (197 x 98½in).*

surface patina that draws attention to stitching, edges and subtle imperfections. Asked what this process means to her, Diana says, 'By dyeing my cloth first, I no longer have "a blank canvas" or "white page" to work with. Removing the dye allows for an element of risk, creates different bleached colours, and a variety of tones and marks related to the printing process; over stitch, this is even more pronounced. In *Handkerchiefs* the different qualities of cloth have resulted in a range of colours all starting from the same black dye.' The subtle differences in the printed surface suggest a patina influenced by and recording the memory of making.

Smaller in scale, she regards her *Boxes* as almost sketchbook-like. Made from found boxes, flattened and worked into with stitch, dye, discharge and print, they help to inform her textile work.

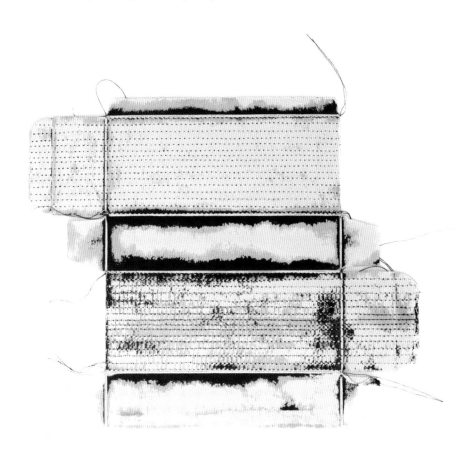

Above: **Box** *by Diana Harrison.*
Stitch, dye, discharge and
screen print on found box.

Alchemy

alchemy: 1 the predecessor of chemistry that aimed to transmute base metals into gold, and create an elixir of everlasting life. 2 transformative processes like alchemy.

Gold has an ancient connection with textiles. Discovered in Roman burials, cloth woven of silk and gold has been dated back to the 4th century AD. From the most primitive beads, feathers, beetle wings and shells to more sophisticated woven metallic textiles, our early ancestors coveted sparkling materials to adorn their bodies and clothing. Embellishments such as these were historically used as talismans to provide magical protection or to imbue the wearer with strength. Commonly though, the use of rich materials was, as today, a symbolic display of wealth and status. Textiles made of gold or silver could easily be liquidated during times of need by throwing the combustible material into a furnace to extract the precious metal. In the medieval royal courts and cathedrals of Europe the dazzling effect of gold and silver, lavishly applied to woven textiles, embroidered costumes, banners and hangings, would have been stunning. Rich and precious materials in this context were used to reinforce a message about the divine rights of the wearer – gold, in this case, symbolizing power and might.

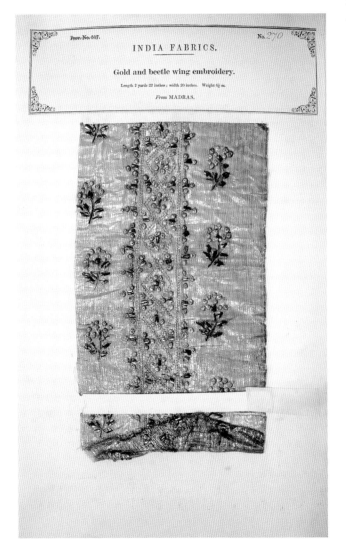

Left: Gold and beetle-wing embroidery in The Textile Fabrics of India Vol VII: Muslins Plain and Embroidered, *c.1866. Bradford College Textile Archive.*

PRECIOUS MATERIALS

What is precious is personal to each of us but by its nature something precious is scarce, and therefore to be coveted and used with care. I tend to use metallic materials sparingly, to emphasize their rarity and special qualities. Here are some of my favourite precious materials to work with.

- Sequins: I particularly love vintage ones made from gelatine, but as they will dissolve in water, textiles embellished with them cannot be washed.
- Glass and metal beads: look for antique ones, or dismantle old beadwork motifs.
- Freshwater pearls and antique 'pearl' shell buttons.
- Found objects: treasures such as pottery shards and freshwater oyster shells.
- Metal threads: modern Lurex threads have their place, while antique silver will beautifully tarnish with time (I generally avoid the glittery threads).
- Metal purl: a continuous spiral of extremely fine wire, usually used in goldwork; the tight coil is used cut into small pieces and threaded through the needle like a bead.
- Metallic silk fabrics: those with a coloured thread in the warp and a silver or metallic across the weft, become beautifully subdued when waxed.

Above: Vintage metal threads, vintage sequins, metal purl, pottery shards, shell fragments, Delica beads.

113

Things that shine, whether of metallic, mineral or organic origin, have always been symbolic of something special. To use these materials says 'this is important', 'this deserves your attention'. On a personal level, we all have our own ideas about what we value highly. For me it is often about the special moments when I experience a beautiful natural phenomenon, like sparkling birdsong, which I chose to represent as a cluster of tiny silver beads in one of my garments for the artwork series *In Search of Green*. For my piece *Baptism*, I used gold stitches and tiny vintage gold sequins to highlight my sense of euphoria from wild swimming and the sensation of cold river water on my skin. The effect of interacting with nature and the elements elicits a sense of awe or elation that is difficult to put into words. Stitches of silver and gold convey something full of wonder, the magical, the transformational. Perhaps this is what medieval alchemists sensed when they claimed that tiny sparks found in the depths of the earth and deep, dark water could be gathered together to create alchemical gold.

Above: Vintage sequins secured with metal purl
act as a highlight on this cyanotype print.

STITCHING WITH SEQUINS

In *Baptism*, I created points of light by stitching on individual vintage sequins. These were secured by using a tiny piece of metal purl, stitched on instead of a bead. Sequins stitched on in this way create a subtle effect just catching the light as pinpoints or highlights.

You will need

- Base fabric of your choice
- Beading needle
- Gold-coloured sewing thread
- Sequins
- Metal purl (smooth purl or check purl)
- Sharp embroidery scissors
- Saucer or small dish to keep sequins and purls from getting lost

Method

1. Cut the purl into short lengths of about 2–3mm.
2. With a knot in the end of the thread, bring your needle up through the fabric where you want the sequin to be placed.
3. Thread on the sequin, followed by a piece of purl.
4. Take the needle back through the hole in the sequin and back through the fabric on the same spot.
5. Repeat as needed. When complete, secure your thread on the back of the work with back stitches or a strong knot.

STITCHING WITH METAL THREADS

Metallic threads have a reputation for being tricky to work with. While they do benefit from a little more care, metallic threads don't have to be difficult to use. Often constructed from a central core of cotton or synthetic fibre, this has a very fine strip of shiny material wrapped around it to give the appearance of a pure metal thread, which can make the outer part of the thread vulnerable to breaking when pulled through the needle or cloth. To prevent this, threads can be waxed using a block of beeswax before stitching, which helps to protect the thread and makes it run through the cloth more smoothly. For thicker metallic threads that would be more difficult to pull through fabric, I often prefer to couch them onto the surface.

The experimental samples shown here demonstrate different ways of working with metallic thread, using plain and decorative stitches as well as couching to create different effects.

Below: Couching is a simple and effective way to work with metallic threads.

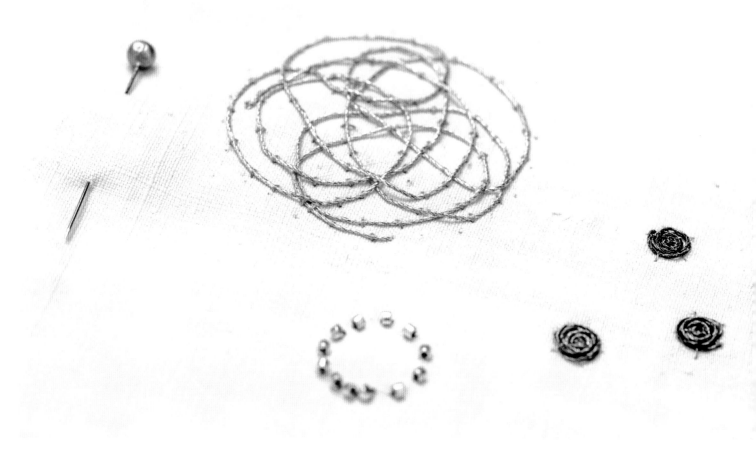

116

Above: Metallic threads have here been threaded between rows of running stitch, leaving a shimmering line of thread on the surface.

Right: Gold cross stitches have been worked on waxed cloth.

Conclusion

TOWARDS A PERSONAL LANGUAGE OF CLOTH

Throughout this book, I have offered my own thoughts about working with cloth to create meaning in my artwork. By sharing these insights I hope to unpick some of the thought processes that happen for me when choosing and working with materials. While cloth has potent symbolic qualities, some of which are shared across cultures, it is important to remember that many meanings can also be highly personal. Finding your own way of working and making personal choices about favoured materials is essential to developing an individual voice for your work. I hope that you will find within this book some things that resonate and encourage you to ask questions in your own practice. An artistic practice is always about finding out about yourself, developing your own personal language of marks, materials and methods, and choosing how to tell your own stories through cloth.

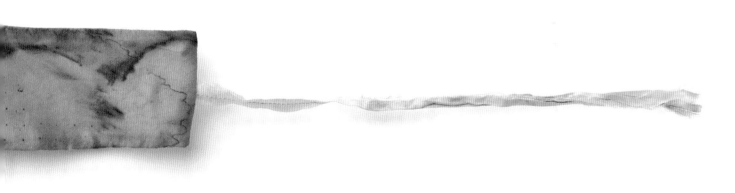

Below: **Home from Home** *(2012).*
A collaborative project with Claire
Wellesley-Smith. Natural dyes,
hand stitch, found materials.

Appendices

FIBRE BURN TEST

A simple burn test can help to determine the fibre content of a fabric. Snip a small piece of your fabric or yarn – just a few centimetres is fine. Place it in a metal tin or tray, or hold it slightly above the tray using tweezers or metal tongs. Ensure you are in a well-ventilated space but away from strong draughts. Make sure there are no other flammable materials nearby. Touch a flame to the fabric and carefully observe the reaction. The table below gives a rough guide to help with identification, but bear in mind that mixed-fibre fabrics may give less conclusive results.

Fibre	Burning	Odour	Residue
Cotton and ramie	Ignites immediately and continues to smoulder once flame is removed. Does not self-extinguish	Burning paper	Small amount of soft grey ash (black ash for mercerized cotton)
Linen, jute and hemp	Ignites quickly and burns rapidly. Does not self-extinguish	Burning grass	Fine, soft grey ash
Rayon/viscose	Ignites on contact. Burns and chars. Does not self-extinguish	Burning paper	Little or no ash
Silk	Draws away from flame. Burns briefly and chars. Self-extinguishing	Burning hair or feathers	Black soft bead, easily crushed (weighted silk will have a lace-like ash)
Wool, cashmere, alpaca	Draws away from flame. Burns briefly and chars. Self-extinguishing	Burning hair or feathers	Dark irregular ash or soft bead – easily crushed
Polyester	Melts before contact with flame. Burns briefly with black smoke. Self-extinguishing	Sweet chemical	Hard black- or cream-coloured bead
Nylon	Draws away from flame and melts. Burns with difficulty. Self-extinguishing	Celery	Hard black- or cream-coloured bead
Acrylic	Melts and burns before contact with flame. Does not self-extinguish	Burning meat/fish/turmeric	Hard bead or irregular ash
Acetate and triacetate	Burns, melts and drips. Does not self-extinguish	Pungent, vinegar	Hard black irregular ash

FURTHER READING

Barnes, Martin. *Shadow Catchers: Camera-less Photography* (Merrell, 2010/2012)

Barnett, P. and Johnson, P. *Textures of Memory: the Poetics of Cloth* (Angel Row Gallery, 1999)

Butler Morrell, A. *The Migration of Stitches & the Practice of Stitch as Movement* (D.S. Mehta/ Sarabhai Foundation, 2007)

Brown, Ruth. *Cyanotypes on Fabric; a Blueprint on How to Produce … Blueprints!* (SC Publications, 2016)

Constantine, Mildred and Reuter, Laurel. *Whole Cloth* (Monacelli Press, 1997)

Franklin, Tracy A. *New Ideas in Goldwork* (Batsford, 2007)

Gordon, Beverly. *Textiles: The Whole Story: Uses, Meaning, Significance* (Thames & Hudson, 2011)

Harris, J. (ed.) *Art_Textiles* (The Whitworth Art Gallery, 2016)

Hewitt, Barbara. *Blueprints on Fabric: Innovative Uses for Cyanotype* (Interweave Press, 1995)

Kettle, Alice and McKeating, Jane. *Hand Stitch: Perspectives* (Bloomsbury, 2012)

Kinnersley-Taylor, Joanna. *Dyeing and Screen-printing on Textiles* (A&C Black, 2nd ed. 2011)

Koren, Leonard. *Wabi-sabi for Artists, Designers, Poets & Philosophers* (Imperfect Publishing, 1994/2008)

Millar, L. (ed.) *Cloth & Memory {2}* (Salts Estates, 2013)

Morrell, Anne. *Using Simple Embroidery Stitches* (Batsford, 1985)

Parrott, Helen. *Mark-making in Textile Art* (Batsford, 2013)

Petersen, Grete and Svennas, Elsie. *Handbook of Stitches* (Batsford, 1970)

Ronnberg, A. and Martin, K. (eds.) *The Book of Symbols: Reflections on Archetypal Images* (Taschen, 2010)

Schoeser, Mary. *Textiles: The Art of Mankind* (Thames & Hudson, 2012)

Tanizaki, Junichiro. *In Praise of Shadows* (1st pub. 1977, new ed. Vintage Classics, 2001)

Wellesley-Smith, Claire. *Slow Stitch: Mindful and Contemplative Textile Art* (Batsford, 2015)

Wellesley-Smith, Claire and Lamb, Hannah. *Lasting Impressions* (Stitch:Print:Weave Press, 2018)

Wood, Sherri Lynn. *The Improv Handbook for Modern Quilters: A Guide to Creating, Quilting & Living Courageously* (STC Craft, 2015)

Suppliers

A few of my favourite shops and suppliers:

New cloth

London
The Cloth House, Misan, Borovick Fabrics, The Silk Society, Soho Silks, Berwick Street Cloth Shop (all on or near Berwick Street, Soho). Within a very short distance you will find a vast range of beautiful fabrics, from fine sheer silks to heavyweight woollens.

Yorkshire
The Shuttle (Shipley). Interesting fabrics including worsted suitings, linens, fancy fabrics, some ex-designer.
Bombay Stores (Bradford) – excellent for silks, metallics and synthetic fabrics. www.bombaystores.co.uk

Mail order
Whaleys (Bradford) Ltd. Wide range of white and undyed fabrics suitable for printing and dyeing, including devoré fabrics, and a really good range of natural fibre fabrics. www.whaleys-bradford.ltd.uk

Old cloth

The Textile Society. Antique and vintage textile fairs held twice each year in London and Manchester: www.textilesociety.org.uk

I also like to rummage at car boot sales, vintage sales and even scrap stores.

Threads & sundries

Barnyarns. Threads and sundries, including soluble fabrics. www.barnyarns.co.uk

Linladan. Vintage linen threads. linladan.com

Golden Hinde. Goldwork supplies. golden-hinde.co.uk

Cyanotype

Silverprint. Raw chemicals and cyanotype kits. www.silverprint.co.uk

Look for photographic suppliers specializing in darkroom supplies and raw chemicals (legislation on the sale and postage of chemicals varies in different countries).

Printing

Colourcraft (C&A) Ltd. Ready-mixed devoré pastes. www.colourcraftltd.com

*Left: Stitch sampler
exploring circular marks.*

Acknowledgements

My heartfelt thanks go to:

The contributing artists.
The staff of Bradford School of Art (Bradford College).
My students and workshop participants for your wise words and observations.
Ruth Brown for teaching me how to apply cyanotype to textiles.
Bradford College Textile Archive.
Chrissie, Lucy, Alice and Claire for your advice and encouragement.

For Mum, who inspired my love of textiles and John for his unwavering faith in me. Thank you for everything.

Image credits

All photography by Michael Wicks except the following: 7, 19, 21, 36, 48, 57 (top and bottom), 59 (top), 60, 64, 66–67, 69, 72, 79, 91, 95, 106, 112 Hannah Lamb; 31 (left) Caroline Bartlett; 37 Claire Wellesley-Smith; 42 (left and right), 43 Leslie Michaelis Onusko; 51 Dawn Jutton; 73 (top) David Rowan; 73 (bottom) Yeshen Venema; 74 Simon Mills; 75 (top and bottom) Freddy Griffiths; 80, 81 (top and bottom) Paul Pavlou; 84, 85 Zoë Hillyard; 96, 97 (top and bottom) Peter Stone; 102, 103 Roger O'Doherty; 108, 109 Debbie Lyddon; 110–111 Diana Harrison.

Winter Forms *(2019).*
Cyanotype and wax on
cotton and linen.

Index

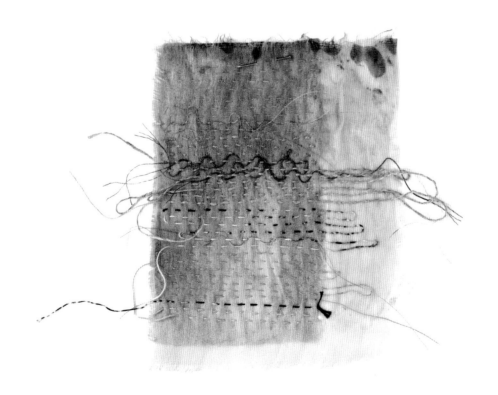

Left: Exploring running stitch and threaded running stitch to create surface textures.